Jim Britt's

Cracking the Rich Code[17]

Inspiring Stories, Insights and Strategies from Top Thought Leaders Around the World

STAY IN TOUCH WITH JIM BRITT

www.JimBritt.com

www.CrackingTheRichCode.com

www.PowerOfLettingGo.com

Cracking the Rich Code[17]

Jim Britt

All Rights Reserved

Copyright 2025

CTRC Publishing and Training, Inc.

10556 Combie Road, Suite 6205

Auburn, CA 95602

The use of any part of this publication, whether reproduced, stored in any retrieval system, or transmitted in any form or by any means, electronic or otherwise, without the prior written consent of the publisher, is an infringement of copyright law.

Jim Britt

Cracking the Rich Code[17]

ISBN:

Co-authors from Around the World

Jim Britt

Cynthia Laden Newman

Kelly Stacey

Robert Ndoping

Jayne Johnson

Ava Diamond Dreyer

Isaac Garcia

Amber McMillan

Steve Higginbotham

Michelle Ihrig

Adam Devito

Reginald G. Jackson, Sr.

Stevi Carr

Corey Poirier

Cheryl Meriot

Huong Nguyen

Marie Zunda

Nathan Baws

Rachel Baws

Melissa Williams-Gurian

Mark Yuzuik

DEDICATION

Entrepreneurs will change the world. They always have and they always will.

Dedicated to the entrepreneurial spirit that lives within each of us. God Bless America and the World!

PREFACE
Jim Britt

In pursuit of a meaningful and fulfilling life, the concept of richness extends far beyond mere financial prosperity. It encompasses a holistic approach, embracing abundance in every facet of our existence—financial, emotional, intellectual, and spiritual. "Cracking the Rich Code with 21 Top Thought Leaders" is not just a manual for accumulating wealth; it is a comprehensive guide to attaining riches in all areas of life.

The journey to holistic riches is a transformative odyssey, and within these pages, you'll find the collective wisdom of 21 experts who have not only achieved remarkable success in their respective field but, have also cracked the code to living a truly rich and fulfilling life, while helping other to do the same. Their stories, insights, and strategies are the keys to unlocking doors to prosperity abundance and well-being.

Our esteemed contributors are visionaries who understand that true richness transcends financial accomplishments. Their perspectives span the spectrum, from business, to personal development, mindfulness, relationships, health and wellness, and spirituality. Each chapter in this book serves as a beacon of guidance, offering a unique perspective on how to navigate the intricate pathways of life to attain richness in all dimensions.

As you delve into the following pages, you'll be introduced to the stories of these remarkable individuals who have not only achieved success in their respective fields, but have also cultivated richness in their relationships, health, and sense of purpose. Their experiences are a testament to the idea that true wealth is a compellation of material prosperity, and the riches found in our connections, personal growth, and the alignment of our actions with our deepest values.

True richness moves beyond the material realm into emotional richness. Emotional intelligence, resilience, and the ability to navigate the complexities of human relationships. Each coauthor offers practical tools and perspectives that will empower you to forge deeper connections, overcome challenges, and find joy in your everyday interactions.

Intellectual richness is also a dimension often overlooked in the pursuit of a rich life. From innovation and creativity to conscious learning and adaptability, intellectual richness is the fuel that propels us forward. All creation begins with an idea. The contributors share their insights into cultivating a curious mind, staying ahead of a rapidly changing world, and leveraging knowledge to create a life of richness and purpose.

Spiritual richness takes center stage too. Beyond religious affiliations, spiritual richness encompasses a profound connection with oneself, others, and the universe. These thought leaders share their journeys of self-discovery, mindfulness, and the pursuit of a higher purpose, offering a more rich and meaningful existence.

This book is not a one-size-fits-all prescription for richness; it a diverse tapestry of ideas, experiences, and strategies that you can tailor to your unique journey. Whether you are an entrepreneur seeking business and financial success, or an individual navigating the complexities of relationships. A lifelong learner, or someone on a spiritual quest, "Cracking the Rich Code" has something for you.

As you embark on this transformative journey with our diverse lineup of thought leaders and experts, just remember that richness is not a destination but a continuous exploration. May the insights and strategies within these pages serve as catalysts for your personal and collective growth, guiding you toward a life of richness in every sense of the word.

Wishing you abundance fulfillment, and richness in all areas of your life.

And remember, just one idea acted upon can change your life. Happy hunting!

Jim Britt

The world's top 50 most influential speakers and top 20 life and success strategist.

www.JimBritt.com

www.CrackingTheRichCode.com

www.PowerOfLettingGo.com

Foreword by Brian Tracy

Life is always a series of transitions... people, places and things that shape who we are as individuals. Often, you never know that the next catalyst for change is just around the corner, in someone you meet, on a page of a book or in a moment of self-reflection.

As the author of 93 books myself, you can imagine how fussy I am to write a foreword to publications in the business and self-development space. My friend Jim Britt is an exception. He has spent decades influencing millions of individuals with his many best-selling books, seminars, programs and coaching, to blossom into the best version of themselves. He has the knowledge, wisdom and skillsets needed to make a significant contribution to overcoming issues entrepreneurs face in business today. His success speaks for itself.

In a world where the pursuit of wealth and success often dominates our collective consciousness, the concept of cracking the rich code has become an elusive quest for many. We marvel at the seemingly effortless success stories of millionaires and billionaires, wondering what secret knowledge or hidden talents they possess that have propelled them to riches. Yet, behind every success story lies a unique and inspiring journey, woven with challenges, triumphs, and invaluable lessons learned.

It is with great excitement that I present to you "Cracking the Rich Code," a book that unveils the remarkable successes of 20 millionaire coauthors. These individuals have not only achieved extraordinary success, but have also generously shared their insights, strategies, and wisdom, inviting the readers to embark on their own transformative journeys.

Within these pages you will discover a variety of stories that defy the myth of an easily attainable overnight success. Instead, you will discover stories of resilience, determination and the unrelenting decisions to pursue their dreams. Each author offers a unique perspective on wealth creation, sharing the secrets they unlocked along their path to financial success.

As you read each chapter you will encounter diverse backgrounds, highlighting the fact that the rich code is not for a certain gender, race, age or social status. You will discover that there are a myriad of ways in which financial success can be achieved.

So, prepare to be inspired as you witness the transformative power of perseverance and the unwavering belief in one's abilities. Through their stories, each coauthor will take you behind the scenes of their successes, allowing you a glimpse into the countless hours of hard work, sacrifices, and failures they encountered along the way.

This book is not just about destination; it's about the journey. Beyond the accumulation of wealth, these authors emphasize the importance of personal growth, finding purpose, and making a positive impact on the world. They share their experience of self-discovery and self-improvement, and offer guidance on developing the mindset, habits, and values necessary to build sustainable success in any and all areas of life.

Their stories will reveal that the rich code is not a hidden secret, but rather a blueprint for anyone willing to embrace the principles with dedication and perseverance. It's about learning from failures, embracing risks, overcoming fears, and continuously expanding one's knowledge and skills. It's about having a mindset of abundance, nurturing relationships, and giving back to society.

Whether you are an aspiring entrepreneur, a seasoned professional, or simply seeking inspiration and guidance, "Cracking the Rich Code" will provide a roadmap to unlocking your real potential. Through the diverse perspectives of Jim Britt and the coauthors, you will find a wealth of actionable strategies, that will empower you to rewrite your own story and chart your course toward financial prosperity.

Let's help in this quest, as Jim Britt and the talented coauthors unselfishly donate their most important asset, their precious

LIFETIME of experience, to elevate one life at a time to their full potential and greatness.

If I were you, I would buy 10 and then giftwrap them to acknowledge your most important top ten relationships in life or clients in business. By doing so, you will strengthen the relationship and encourage others to live a more fulfilling life.

As you close the pages of any of the books in this series, you will gain a new life of clarity and focus as never before. *Cracking the Rich Code* will provide tools to transform results for corporations, institutions, and individuals, both personally and financially.

If you've ever wanted to read a book that challenges you to become more than you are and leaves you with enough inspiration to last a lifetime, *Cracking the Rich Code* is it!

Allow all you have read in this book to create introspection and redirection if required.

Remember, death is certain. Success is not. This life is your journey to craft.

Brian Tracy

Table of Content

Foreword by Brian Tracy xi
Jim Britt 1
   Think Like Superman
Ava Diamond Dreyer 13
   Optimizing The Rich Code
Kelly Stacey 23
   From Slipping Through the Cracks to Cracking the Rich Code
Adam DeVito 33
   The Inspired Leader: The Inner Path to Growth & Success
Isaac Garcia 49
   It's Just Not Working Anymore
Nathan Baws 61
   The Dopamine-Driven Business Builder
Rachel Baws 75
   From Candy Negotiations to Real Estate Millions
Steve Higginbotham 87
   BeYouToFull
Reginald G. Jackson, Sr. 97
   Align Your Focus with Your Intention
Stevi Gable Carr 105
   Audacious By Design: 6 Audacious Acts to Fuel Legacy Through Well-being

Huong Nguyen **119**
Success with peace of mind – Building wealth in JOY: Where achievement is harmoniously aligned with inner peace and happiness.

Michelle Mueller Ihrig **131**
Navigating by Heart

Corey Poirier **141**
The Power of Synchronicity

Marie Zunda **149**
Soul Reflections to THRIVE

Melissa Williams-Gurian **157**
What Do Feelings Have to Do with Business? Everything!

Robert Ndoping **169**
Resilience: A Journey to Find Purpose

Cynthia Laden Newman **177**
Looking Back: A Life Shaped by Challenges and Opportunities

Amber McMillan **191**
Worth Ethic: Redefining Work Ethic Through the Lens of Self-Worth

Jayne Johnson **201**
How You Create an Upward Spiral of Success: The 8 Elements of A Game Blueprint

Cheryl Meriot **213**
Unwritten: A Journey Through Control, Chaos, and Coming Home to Myself

Nina Buik **223**
Lunch with a side of Transformation

Afterword **231**

Jim Britt

Jim Britt is an award-winning author of fifteen #1 International best-sellers. Some of his many titles include Rings of Truth, Do This. Get Rich-For Entrepreneurs, Unleashing Your Authentic Power, The Power of Letting Go, Cracking the Rich Code Series and The Entrepreneur.

Jim is an internationally recognized business and life strategist who is highly sought after as a keynote speaker, both online and live, for all audiences.

As an entrepreneur Jim has launched 28 successful business ventures. He has served as a success strategist to over 300 corporations worldwide and is one of the world's top 50 most influential speakers and top 20 life and business success strategists. He was presented with the "Best of the Best" award out of the top 100 contributors of all time to the Direct Selling industry.

For over four decades Jim has presented seminars throughout the world sharing his success strategies and life enhancing realizations with over 5,000 audiences, totaling almost 2,000,000 people from all walks of life.

Early in his speaking career he was in business with the late Jim Rohn for eight years, where Tony Robbins worked under Jim's direction for his first few years in the speaking business.

As a performance strategist, Jim leverages his skills and experience as one of the leading experts in peak performance, entrepreneurship and personal empowerment to produce stellar results. He is pleased to work with small business entrepreneurs, and anyone seeking to remove the blocks that stop their success in any area of their life.

One of Jim's latest programs "Cracking the Rich Code" focuses on the subconscious programs influencing one's relationship with money and their financial success. www.CrackingTheRichCode.com

Think Like Superman

By Jim Britt

"Waking up to your true greatness in life requires letting go of who you imagine yourself to be."

--- Jim Britt

FACT: Becoming a millionaire is easier than it has ever been.

Many people have the notion that it's an impossible task to become a millionaire. Some say, "It's pure luck." Others say, "You have to be born into a rich family." For others, "You'll have to win the Lotto." And for many, they say, "Your parents have to help you out a lot." That's the language of the poor.

A single mother with five children says, "I want to believe in what you're saying. However, I'm 45 years old and work long hours at two dead-end jobs. I barely earn enough to get by. What should I do?"

Another man said, "Well, if you work for the government, you cannot expect to become a millionaire. After all, you're on a fixed salary and there's little time for anything else. By the time you get home, you've got to play with the kids, eat dinner, and fall asleep watching TV."

Everyone has a story as to why they could never become a millionaire. But for every story, excuse really, there are other stories OR PEOPLE with worse circumstances that have become rich.

The truth is that all of us can become as wealthy as we decide to be, and that's a mindset. None of us is excluded from wealth. If you have the desire to receive money, whatever the amount, you have all of the rights to do so like everyone else. There is no limit to how much you can earn for yourself. The only limitations are what you place on yourself.

Money is like the sun. It does not discriminate. It doesn't say, "I will not give light and warmth to this flower, tree, or person because I don't like them." Like the sun, money is abundantly available to all of us who truly believe that it is for us. No one is excluded.

There are, however, some major differences between rich and poor people. Here are some tips for becoming rich.

Change Your Thinking

You have to see the bigger picture. There are opportunities everywhere! The problem is that most people see just trees when they should be looking at the entire forest. By doing so, you will see that there are opportunities everywhere. The possibilities are endless.

You'll also have to go through plenty of self-discovery before you earn your first million. Knowing the truth about yourself isn't always the easiest task. Sometimes, you'll find that you are your biggest enemy—at least some days.

Learn from Millionaires

Most people are surrounded by what I like to call their "default friends." These friends are acquaintances that we see at the gym, school, work, local happy hour, and other places. We naturally befriend these people because we are all in the same boat financially. However, these people aren't millionaires in most cases and cannot help you become one either. In fact, if you tell them, you will become a millionaire, some may even tell you that it's impossible and discourage you from even trying. They'll tell you that you're living in a fantasy world and why you'll never be able to make it happen. Instead, learn from millionaires. Let go of these relationships that pull you down regarding your money desires. It's okay to have friends that aren't millionaires. However, only take input from those who have accomplished what you want to accomplish. Hang out with those who will encourage and help you reach the next level. Don't give your raw diamonds to a bricklayer to cut.

Indulge in Wealth

To become wealthy, you must learn about wealth. This means that you'll have to put yourself in situations that you've never been in before.

ON OCCASION, DO SOME OF THESE:

Fly first class and see how it makes you feel.

Eat out at the finest restaurant, and don't look at the price on the menu.

Take a limo instead of a cab or Uber. Watch how you feel.

Reserve a suite in a first-class hotel.

If you are used to drinking a $20 bottle of wine, go for the $100 and see how it tastes. It does taste different.

All I am saying is, try some things that wealthy people do and see how it makes you feel.

Believe it is Possible

If you believe it is possible to become a millionaire, you can make it happen. However, if you've excluded yourself from this possibility and think and believe that it's for other people, you'll never become a millionaire.

Also, be sure to bless rich people when you can. Haters of money aren't likely to receive any of it either.

Read books that millionaires have written. By gaining a well-rounded education about earning large sums of money and staying inspired, you'll be able to learn the wealth secrets of the rich. I just saw a video on LinkedIn with my friend Kevin Harrington from the TV show Shark Tank. He said that one of his new companies just had a million-dollar day on Amazon.

Enlarge Your Service

Your material wealth is the sum of your total contribution to society. Your daily mantra should be, *'How do I deliver more value to more people in less time?'* Then, you'll know that you can always increase your quality and quantity of service. Enlarging your service is also about going the extra mile. When it comes to helping others, you must give everything you have. You just plant the seeds, and nature will take care of the rest.

Seize ALL Opportunities That Make Sense

You cannot say "No" to opportunities and expect to become a millionaire. You must seize every opportunity that has your name on it. It may just be an opportunity to connect with an influential person for no reason. Sometimes the monetary reward will not come immediately, but if you keep planting seeds, eventually, you'll grow a fruitful crop. Money is the harvest of the service you provide and sometimes the connections you have. The more seeds you plant, the greater the harvest.

Have an Unstoppable Mindset

Want to know some of what my first mentor shared with me that took me from a broke factory worker, a high school dropout, to a millionaire?

First, he said, you must start thinking like a wealthy, unstoppable person. You must have a wealth mindset. He said that wealthy people think differently. He said, "I want you to start thinking like Superman!" Sounds crazy, right? Well, it's not. It's powerful, and here's why. How you think will change your life.

Wealthy people think differently. They really do. And anyone can learn to think like the wealthy.

I'm not talking about positive thinking, the Law of Attraction, or motivation. Let's get real. None of that stuff works anyway. Otherwise, we would all be prosperous and happy already. Instead, I'm talking about thinking based on quantum physics. Once you understand and apply it, it will change your life. You will become unstoppable!

If there was any fictional or real person whose qualities you could instantly possess, who would that person be? Think about it. Personally, I would say that Superman is the perfect person. Now, you are probably thinking I have lost it, right? Just stick with me here. You will like what you are about to hear.

Superman is a fictional superhero widely considered one of the most famous and popular action heroes and an American cultural icon. I remember watching Superman every Saturday morning when I was a kid. I couldn't get enough. He was my hero!

Let's look at Superman's traits:

Superman is indestructible.

He is a man of steel.

He can stop a locomotive in its tracks.

Bullets bounce off him.

He is faster than a speeding bullet.

No one can bring him down.

He can leap tall buildings in a single bound. Great powers to have in this day and age, wouldn't you say? What else would you need?

Now, for all you females, don't worry. We have not left you out. There is also a female version of Superman named Superwoman. She has the same powers as Superman.

Now, this is where it gets interesting. Let's first look at the qualities that Superman possesses that you want to make your own. And to make it simple, I will refer to Superman for the rest of this message, and you can replace him with Superwoman if you are female.

Again:

Superman is powerful and fearless.

Superman is virtually indestructible—except for kryptonite, of course.

Superman can stop bullets.

Superman has supernatural powers. He can see through walls.

Superman can stop a speeding locomotive.

Superman can stop a bullet.

Superman jumps into immediate action when troubles arise.

Superman can crash through barriers.

Superman can even change clothes in a phone booth in seconds. Not too many of those around anymore. You'll have to duck behind a building to change.

So, you're thinking right now, 'Okay, I know that Superman has incredible supernatural powers, how can that help me? What good will it do me to think I am Superman, a fictional character?'

Here is where science comes in. This is the part where you will be amazed when you learn about the supernatural powers you already possess! NO, REALLY!

Your brain makes certain chemicals called neuropeptides. These are literally the molecules of emotion, like love, fear, joy, passion, etc. These molecules of emotion are not only contained in your brain but circulate throughout your cellular structure. They send out a signal, a frequency much like a radio station sending out a signal. For example, you tune in to 92.5, and you get jazz. Tune in to 99.6, and you get rock. And if you are just one decimal off, you get static. The difference is that your signal goes both ways. You are a sender and a receiver.

You put out a signal, a mindset of confidence about your financial success, and people, circumstances, and opportunities show up to support your success. When you put out a signal of doubt and uncertainty, you receive support for your doubt and uncertainty. You've been around someone you didn't trust or felt less than positive just being in their presence, right? You have also been around people that inspire you. That's what I'm talking about. You are projecting a frequency, looking to resonate with the frequency you are transmitting.

Anyway, the amazing part about these cells of emotion is that they are intelligent. They are thinking cells. These cells are constantly eavesdropping on the conversation that you are having with yourself. That's right. They are listening to you! And others are listening to your cells as well. Others feel what you feel when they are around you.

Your unconscious mind and cells are listening in, waiting to adjust your behavior based on what they hear from you, their master. So just imagine what would happen if you started thinking like Superman or a millionaire.

Here are some of the thoughts you might have during the day:

"The challenges I face today are easily overcome, after all I am Superman."

"I am indestructible."

"I have incredible strength."

"Nothing can stop me...NOTHING."

"I have supernatural powers and can overcome anything."

"I can accomplish anything I want when I put my mind to it."

"I can break through any barrier."

"I can and I will do whatever it takes to accomplish my goal."

"I fear nothing."

The trillions of thinking cells in your body and brain listen, and they create exactly what you tell them to create. Their mission is to complete the picture of the you they see and hear when you talk to them. They must obey. It's their job!

Since you are Superman, you cannot fail. Why? Your thinking cells are now sending the proper signal because you told them to. They are making you stronger and more successful every day! You have the ability to fight off all negativity, doubt, fear, and worry—nothing can stop you!

Superman has total confidence. So, your cells of emotion relating to confidence will now create more neuropeptide chemicals to promote feelings of power and confidence that others will feel in your presence.

Superman is fearless. So, your cells of emotion relating to fear will now create more neuropeptide chemicals to create feelings of courage. You are unstoppable!

And here's the key. Others will respond to you in the same way that you are talking to yourself.

If you are confident, others will have confidence in you.

You have thousands of thoughts every day. Make sure your thoughts are leading you in the direction you want to go. Ensure you tell your cells a success story and not a 'woe is me' story.

Most have been conditioned to think that creating wealth is difficult or only for the lucky few. What do you believe? It doesn't cost anything to think like Superman, and it is much more inspiring!

Mediocrity cannot be an option if you decide to be wealthy and think like Superman.

Your decision and communication with your cells create a mindset; that influences how you show up.

None of that old type of thinking matters anymore. After all, you are Superman, and you can accomplish anything.

If you want wealth, you have to stretch yourself. You have to do the things that unsuccessful people are unwilling to do. You have to say "yes" to an opportunity, then figure out how to get the job done.

Maybe you are uncomfortable selling and asking for money. If that's the case, then learn sales and learn to ask for money every day until you feel comfortable asking for it. You will never have money if you don't learn to ask for it.

I've learned a lot in the past 40+ years as an entrepreneur. I've learned that in order to have more, you have to become more. I've also learned that if you are comfortable, you are not growing. I realized that I couldn't go from being a nervous rookie speaker with minimal self-confidence to hosting TV shows and speaking in front of 5,000 people overnight. I simply wasn't ready. I grew into that, one speaking engagement at a time. Every time I finished a speaking engagement, I would ask myself, "How did I do it, and how could I do it better?" I still do that today.

And I've learned from the hundreds of thousands of people I've trained, coached, and mentored that none of us can do something we don't believe is possible. It won't happen if you're not ready to step out of your comfort zone and stretch yourself.

This has led me to understand the most important principle of wealth-building, which has meant the difference between poverty and riches for people since humans first traded for pelts.

Are you ready?

Come in just a little closer. Listen up!

Every income level requires a different you, a different mindset! If you think that $10,000 a month is a lot of money, then $100,000 a month will be completely out of reach. If you believe that having $5,000 in the bank would make you rich, then $50,000 won't miraculously appear. You will never earn more money than you believe is "a lot" of money.

What you do as a business is only a small part of becoming rich. In fact, there are thousands, if not tens of thousands, of ways to make money—and lots of it. I've learned over the years that focusing on who you want to become instead of what you need to do will multiply your chances of getting rich a hundredfold.

Ask anyone who's found a way to make a large sum of money legally, and they will tell you that it's not hard once you crack the code. And cracking the code starts with you and your mindset. The "code" I refer to isn't a secret rite or ancient scroll. It's not even a secret. It's a certain way of thinking and believing in which you've trained your mind to see money-making ideas.

That's where you see a need in the marketplace and jump on the idea quickly. It might involve creating a new product, or it may just be teaching others a special technique you've learned. It may even require raising capital to start a company or to market a product or idea on social media.

Don't Hold Back. You Have to Take Action to Change.

Start right now to imagine yourself as already having wealth. How would your life be? How would your day unfold? Start to own your wealth mindset now! The subconscious mind is unable to differentiate between fact and mere visualization. So, by imagining that you already have it, you're encouraging your subconscious mind to seek the ways and means to transform your imaginary feelings into the real thing.

Find yourself some mentors. Nobody has all the answers. Surround yourself with people who will support, inspire, and provide solutions that keep you moving in the right direction. Having a qualified mentor is essential if you genuinely want to attain wealth, have a thriving business, or reach the top of your game in any endeavor.

Okay, let's come in for a landing…

Having a crystal-clear picture of what you want to accomplish is essential before you begin. If you want to attain wealth, you must learn to operate without fear and with a sharply defined mental image of the outcome you want to attain. This comes from thinking like a wealthy person (like Superman), making decisions like a wealthy person, and being fearless (like Superman) when stepping out of your comfort zone. Look at the result as something you're already prepared to do; you just haven't done it yet.

Think about this. You have been preventing your success; it's not something you have to struggle to make happen. The key is not letting fear, doubt, other people, or mind chatter push your success away. You'll find that the solutions taking you toward your goals will come to you in the most unexpected and sudden ways. You don't need the *perfect* plan first. You need a perfectly clear decision about your success, the right mindset, mentoring, and the ideal way to get you there will materialize.

The most significant transfer of wealth in the history of the human race is happening right now. Are you positioned to get your share?

Remember, in order to get a different result, you must do something different. In order to do something different, you must know something different to do. And in order to know something different, you have to first suspect that your present methods need improving.

THEN, YOU HAVE TO BE WILLING TO DO SOMETHING ABOUT IT.

***

To contact Jim:

For more information on Jim's work:

www.JimBritt.com

http://JimBrittCoaching.com

www.facebook.com/jimbrittonline

www.linkedin.com/in/jim-britt

For free audio series sessions 1&2 www.PowerOfLettingGo.com

Ava Diamond Dreyer

Ava Diamond Dreyer, LCSW, Therapist, Athlete, Facilitator, Creator of Brain Optimization Coaching, Brain Care Bootcamp, and The Optimized Lawyer, is a BioPsychoSocial Entrepreneur.

I do things backwards often, know how to think "outside the box" but also BE "the box", and a believer in simplifying success through neuroscience. While I have credentials from prestigious schools behind my name, the credibility that matters are the words of appreciation from thousands of clients throughout my 30+ (oy) years carving my niche and fulfilling my vision in the wellness/performance space. I have implemented my programs at Yale University School of Medicine, with leaders in our US Military, professional athletes, in Fortune 100 companies, major hospitals, and top global law firms. I've had the joy of sharing what I have assimilated into Brain Optimization Coaching through top podcasts and articles, including CNBC. It was cool to be recognized in the "Top 15 Coaches in New York City" by Influencer Magazine.

I know firsthand how hard life can be and how to thrive through ordeals. I have raised three children to be life-valuing "Overcomers" as adults. I have married a man who believes in the power of possibility. I surround myself with soulful people who keep it real. At this point in my life, my greatest responsibility is to fulfill my role as a community member by doing my small part regularly to move the needle even just a little bit toward betterment.

Optimizing The Rich Code

By Ava Diamond Dreyer

There are probably a number of great reasons why you have chosen Cracking the Rich Code as your next read. Whichever reason is yours likely depends on how you define "rich."Financial wealth doesn't automatically equate to happiness, health, or fulfillment. Of course, it can make acquiring some of those things a whole lot easier. In my personal and professional experiences coaching thousands of people over the past 30 years, I've witnessed those in the top 2% and the bottom 2% of the socioeconomic bracket struggling with the same issues that make them feel "poor." The former are just able to mask the problems better. The common denominator was addiction to something that robbed them of far more than their money. Addiction cost them relationships, jobs, and integrity. They suffered a severe disconnect from themselves and from others.

One of the game-changing truths that I discovered is that every human brain is addicted to patterns in order to make sense of things. Sometimes, those patterns, while they begin as helpful tools, become interferences or worse. A second truth is that every human brain craves control. It's how we ward off threats. Combining the pattern and control concepts, it's easier to realize how we can wind up on autopilot with limiting beliefs and behaviors. It's easier to remain in thought patterns than recognize and adjust them to serve us better.

My clients were trapped in a cycle of thinking, feeling, and doing and desperately wanted to crack that code to a richer life marked by various shades of honor. The problem was not one code worked for everyone. Treatment programs failed over and over again for so many. Support groups weren't right for others. There was something missing and my mission was to uncover what it was that filled the gap. My purpose and passion were aligned in creating a new approach to healthier, "wealthier" life. I dubbed myself a "BioPsychoSocial Entrepreneur" as I allowed my entrepreneurial bent to amalgamate all I had learned formally and with experience in biological sciences, psychological theories, and social dynamics.

This is where my deep dive into the workings of the brain began. For the next 12 years, I researched, studied, and practiced a neuroscience approach to protecting and promoting all of our energies: cognitive, emotional, physical, and spiritual. I developed resilience training for young docs at Yale University School of Medicine. This was the seed that grew into Brain Optimization Coaching.

There are a few things that I am willing to wager you already know: Walking is good for you. Eating vegetables is important. Breathing helps. Mindfulness and meditation are calming. Going to another stress-management seminar will mean hearing the same old things and doing nothing more with them. Success is in your grasp with mere dedication and hard work, right?

I am also willing to wager that even if you are well-educated and worldly, you don't already know that:

1. Chronic Stress is the primary trigger for more injuries and illnesses than any other condition.
2. Two minutes can do a ton of good for your wellness & performance.
3. The symptoms of poor BRAIN nutrition and depression are identical.
4. The best mindset is NOT always using positive thinking.
5. Your imagination is your greatest stress-management tool.
6. When your brain is not properly hydrated, it actually shuts down in parts.
7. How you handle the first fifteen minutes of waking up can improve your entire day.

Brain care is foundational to all of your self-care and performance efforts. Without it, nothing else you do for self-care or performance will work nearly as well. When facilitating workshops, I often ask participants this significant question: "Did you brush your teeth today?" (Always lots of giggles and nods…and, by the way, if there are more than 20 people in the room then at least one person is lying.) Which is then followed by the more important question, "Why?" You can probably guess the top few answers. Most people can state their reasons for teeth brushing pretty easily because it is a solid habit thanks to good parenting long ago. The last question on this topic of teeth is, "Could anyone convince you not to brush your teeth before you leave the house?" Teeth brushing is a non-negotiable for most. My mission is to help millions of people care for their brains as regularly as they care for their teeth to prevent decay, preserve functionality, and promote "fresh" energies.

When Jim Britt and I had our conversation about joining the team of experts for this edition of Cracking the Rich Code, it made perfect sense to secure a chapter at the beginning of the book so that you can make the most of the unique insights and strategies shared in each subsequent chapter. With Brain Optimization strategies, we become **R.I.C.H.** (**R**esilient, **I**ntegrous, **C**onnected, and **H**opeful)! When we are Optimized, we can perceive and receive what we need better. We are clearer, calmer, and more confident. We can absorb, problem-solve, create, and engage better. With this as the primary focus and having a single chapter in this great book, I will give you a few key strategies that can help you glean the golden nuggets you need for curating your own Rich Code.

After the oral hygiene series, my only question is, "Are you open to Optimizing?" If yes, here is your introduction to the four pillars of Brain Optimization: Nutritional Psychology, Mindset, Movement, and Restoration.

NUTRITIONAL PSYCHOLOGY

As a former professional fitness competitor, I can talk about diet for muscle development and fat loss all day long. I don't. My focus is on what we eat and when we eat it to positively impact our quality of life, longevity, and productivity. It's a shame that so many doctors who are prescribing medications for depression, anxiety, sleep, concentration problems, sex drive issues, etc., don't talk with patients about their nutritional intake. There is extensive research supporting how nutrients can positively affect all of those areas of the human experience. Email me if you want a list, and I will gladly send you studies. For those who do need pharmaceuticals, did you know that what you eat can help or hinder the efficacy of your medications? Why wouldn't we use foods to manage mood, energy, focus, and sleep quality first or in conjunction with other efforts?

Our brain doesn't know the difference between internal stress and external stress. Elevated cortisol maintained for longer than two weeks damages our entire system. It causes congestion of dead cells in your brain that thwarts your ability to learn and remember. It causes digestive issues, fat loss challenges, and emotional dysregulation. Cortisol causes wear and tear on our entire system, triggering more injuries and illnesses than any other condition.

We need to enjoy food and redefine "diet" to be about how nutrients protect & promote our cognitive, emotional, and physical energies. I'm glad that people are paying more attention to the gut:brain axis, cortisol levels, illness and injury factors, etc. that have inflammation as their marker for needing help. The primary and most essential element to putting out inflammation is water. If the brain is 4 oz shy of what it needs, it goes dormant in parts. Which parts? The ones that it deems not necessary for "survival." Creativity, concentration, and memory go into deficit. Hydration is key to neurogenesis (replenishment of brain cells) and neuroplasticity (the ability to generate new brain connections). Stabilizing blood sugar is also essential to brain functioning. Those who struggle with concentration and anxiety will worsen with blood sugar spikes and dips. Nutrient-dense snacks and meals help you to stay off that internal roller coaster of energy and, consequently, reduce inflammation.

- Hydrate. Minimally eleven 8-oz glasses of water and ideally closer to fourteen! **RICH CODE TIP**: Be sure to drink a full glass a few minutes before you start reading.

- Keep blood sugar stable with nutrient-dense foods eaten every 3 hours. Stabilizing snack tips: sweet potato, oatmeal, healthy fat (natural nut butter or avocado) on dark, grainy bread. **RICH CODE TIP**: No large meals or simple carbohydrates just before or as you read.

- Eliminate processed foods.

- Cognitive performance-enhancing diet: Mind/DASH Diet combined, Mediterranean Diet, NASA Diet, The Blue Zones Diet.

MINDSET

One of my pet peeves when supervising therapists and other wellness providers is when they tell their clients to "just think positively." If they could do that, they didn't need an appointment. When we are struggling with sad or anxious thoughts, the most effective way to calm that energy is to neutralize it with facts. The brain doesn't like to be lied to, and sometimes there is nothing "positive" to say about a situation. That said, there are always facts that can empower us. To generate a solid go-to list of neutralizing facts about yourself, you will assess your "Core Powers." Before we understand what those are, let me first share why those are needed.

Again, our brain is designed to protect us. It tries to make sense of things to ease stress and pave our path forward. To do so, it acts like Google. When you start to type into your Google search bar, Google will most often finish your sentence and give you a bunch of options to click. When a situation (or thought) is "typed in" to your brain, it automatically searches for the most commonly used or dominant memory response. Our efficient brain comes to quick conclusions about what something must mean and how you should feel. Mindset is formed and fueled by triggers and responses in our brain. This pattern can actually distort perception both in the moment and in memory.

The words we use to ourselves and out loud also shape our perception. We see life and our reflection based on the neurolinguistic programming in our brain. This is why a group of people can experience the same situation and describe it differently. It's why siblings raised together have different memories about childhood family life. When we consciously choose language rather than running on autopilot, we can absolutely optimize our cognitive and emotional energies. We can find our footing, problem-solve better, and develop Realistic Optimism. Realistic Optimism takes into account the negatives while trusting we can thrive through to a better place. Mindset can keep us stuck with autopilot responses or scaffold us with the power of possibilities. We can direct the thought traffic more easily than most realize.

Brain trickery can help mitigate stress. One of Brain Optimization's stress-reduction strategies is grounded in the evidence-based practice of visualization but coupled with the forgotten power of imagination. When we are kids, our imagination serves us well in exploring what it would be like to have superpowers, imaginary friends, and toys come to life and be grown-ups. As we develop, we erroneously let go of this incredible tool that the human mind owns. Sadly, those who endure trauma "escape" from it with this same mechanism. Our imagination can be a way out of daily stress, too. Visualization techniques (while often not done properly) are incredibly effective in rewiring neural pathways to reduce anxieties and forge better associations with situations when done right. With the information above, the following strategies are designed to allow you to work with the protective mechanisms of your brain without giving your brain free reign over your perception and emotions.

- Make a short and reliable list of your Core Powers. Your Core Powers are those values, beliefs, personality traits, and skills. Consider what allows you to show up in any of your roles in life feeling good, capable, and authentic. Find two in each category. When grappling with a mindset that keeps you spiraling in various shades of fear, anchor yourself with one or more of your Core Powers. Consciously choose a Core Power or two to lead your thoughts and behaviors. With rehearsal, you will recondition your neural pathways so that a trigger will lead to a Core Power response. **RICH CODE TIP**: before reading, take one minute to ground yourself in your Core Powers. As you read, it will shift your mindset to being less reactive and more open to new ideas.

- The Peaceful Place exercise combines imagination and sensory stimulation. It proves highly effective in lowering cortisol and calming the central nervous system. When feeling overwhelmed, engage the power of imagination by recalling the most peaceful place you've been (anything from your bed to your favorite beach to your grandmother's kitchen… as long as there are no negative associations with the place, too). Using all of your senses, imagine being there. Be there for a few minutes and notice where it resonates most in your being. Focus on that part. **RICH CODE TIP:** To create open-mindedness as you read, do the Peaceful Place exercise just before picking up this book.

MOVEMENT

Aside from daily exercise, there is a kind of movement that must happen throughout a day to optimize wellness & performance alike. Every human brain has rhythms. Most of us know of the Circadian Rhythm (if we didn't skip class that day in high school). Most of us don't know about the Ultradian Rhythm, however. These are cycles of cognitive energy, and while they do range individually, no brain is designed to be in focused mental work mode for longer than two hours. When people muscle through that time frame, damage begins with the build-up of cortisol-crushed brain cells. Our brain goes into fight-or-flight mode and starts to go dormant. It's like when your devices go into battery-saving mode. We want to protect, preserve, and promote our energies. There is no benefit or reward for running on empty.

The 242 Strategy: This one is key to optimizing brain functioning, metabolism, heart wellness, mood, and more. The 242 Strategy is designed to flush out those dead cells and replenish cognitive energy. Clients report an incredible difference in how they approach and complete their work when they implement 242 consistently. 242 is two minutes of intentional movement for every two hours of focused mental work. Intentional movement is moving just for the sake of moving (for self-care & performance). It's separate from having to grab a coffee or hit the restroom. Intentional movement can be walking (outside best), dancing to your favorite song (equal best), stretching, mat pilates, floor exercises, sprints, etc. **RICH CODE TIP**: Just do it, and even if you are so engrossed in this fabulous read, set your timer for two minutes.

RESTORATION

Restoring brain chemistry balance comprehensively relies on longer decompression strategies. While many can't have adequate sleep hours nightly, they can have quality sleep that helps with restoration. Restoration also happens through Flow-State activities (those things that you do for enjoyment and wind up losing track of time). It is essential to your entire physical system to create space for healing and rejuvenation. While vacations are wonderful, there is often the pre-vacation stress of "getting everything done" and preparing whatever is needed in our absence and the pre-return angst of "what is waiting for me" when we return home. Brain Optimization strategies for Restoration are designed to put a little vacation for your mind and body in every single day. For the sake of this chapter's focus, however, I will give you a strategy that can create an opportunity for a more impactful reading method.

Digital Detox: Choose a minimum of three hours to completely disconnect from technology. Strive to increase that window until you have one full day of digital detox. I can't wait for you to feel what happens mentally and physically! **RICH CODE TIP:** Enjoy and absorb reading even more during your dedicated time without technology.

The aforementioned ideas and lifestyle strategies will give you a great start to an Optimized experience. That said, there is one additional strategy that I really want you to have now. It is truly one of the most influential methods to Healthy Control. How you do daybreak can make or break the rest of your day. You may be familiar with Robin Sharma's book, "The 5 AM Club." The concept behind it is famous and inspiring, but, as I learned through firsthand and client experiences in the thousands, it is not necessary to do it for an hour as the sun rises. In fact, the benefits of taking charge of how you begin each day can be profoundly experienced at any time you wake and in only 15 minutes.

Daybreak 555: Before you look at your email, social media, text messages, or turn on the TV, gift yourself a wake-up routine that puts you in charge of your energies. I promise this one is a life-bettering practice you will want to share with everyone you love (or even like).

5 minutes of Cognitive Nourishment: Listen to or read about something that is NOT in your typical wheelhouse of need-to-know topics. This is a want-to-know kind of cognitive nourishment.

5 minutes of Physical Nourishment: Simply connect with your physical self. I like to do a 5-minute kettlebell workout or mobility training. Stretching, muscle activation techniques, or a walk around your yard all work, too.

5 minutes of Spiritual Nourishment: Take five minutes to activate your hope, integrity (Core Powers as above), gratitude, nature, or prayer.

The hardest part of contributing to this masterpiece of a book was trying to give you everything that I wanted to give in 3000 words. My Rich Code activates the blend of my purpose, passion, and power to elevate life with others. I practice what I preach, live what I teach, and reap the invaluable reward of helping others master wellness and performance alike.

Let me know what you discovered to be YOUR Rich Code!

***

To contact Ava:

Linkedin: www.linkedin.com/in/avadiamondoptimized

Web site: www.BrainOptimized.com

Email: Ava@BrainOptimized.com

Kelly Stacey

Kelly Stacey is a wife, mother, and grandmother with a passion for lifelong learning and personal growth. With over 20 years of experience transforming brands into multi-million-dollar enterprises, she has collaborated with more than 300 brands, creating momentum for both emerging and established businesses. Today, Kelly helps entrepreneurs, founders, and leaders conquer the constraints holding them back and achieve new heights of success.

After overcoming a childhood marked by loss and adversity, Kelly transformed her challenges into steppingstones, building a career focused on empowerment and resilience. Her journey has inspired others to rewrite their stories, break generational cycles, and reach their true potential.

Driven to support entrepreneurs with limited resources, Kelly founded a Skool community for founders and start-ups. This innovative platform provides essential tools, resources, and guidance to help emerging businesses thrive, even without significant financial backing.

At home, Kelly cherishes time with her family and enjoys watching her daughter play collegiate soccer at Southern Nazarene University. She finds balance in Pilates, yoga, and personal development through reading and podcasts. Her guiding philosophy is simple yet profound: "Meet your potential and encourage others along the way."

Now in her early fifties, Kelly focuses on empowering others through her work, coaching, and storytelling, proving that courage and authenticity can crack any code to success.

From Slipping Through the Cracks to Cracking the Rich Code

By Kelly Stacey

I've always been afraid of dark water and slipping through the cracks. You know, those cracks you see when you walk on a pier? I mean, what's in that dark water? Whatever it is, I want no part of it.

That was me most of my life—worrying about "slipping through the cracks." My story isn't unique, though. It's one that many can relate to. My mother passed away in a car accident when I was eight years old. She was 28 and left behind three little girls and her high school sweetheart—my dad. She was the fourth oldest of eight and was raised by alcoholic parents. My dad was raised by his grandmother. His father was physically abusive to both my dad and his mother.

The year leading up to my mom's passing was very tumultuous, to say the least. My parents separated as my mom struggled with alcohol. She moved out and left me and my sisters with my dad. Abandonment comes to mind. That year, they both dated other people. My mom continued to struggle with alcohol and made some massive mistakes along the way. All the while, my sisters and I were along for the emotional ride and exposed to some very traumatic events.

After my mom passed away, my dad quickly remarried. My stepmom was a controlling and verbally abusive person. She said horrible things about my mom, which further deepened the wounds. She forbade us to see our mom's family. So, on top of losing our mom, we lost the only family we ever knew. They divorced when I was thirteen.

The sense of isolation became a defining feature of my early years. It shaped my perception of safety and connection, making it hard to trust anyone fully. By the time I reached adolescence, I was a walking anxiety time bomb. That's the condensed summary of my childhood years.

Fast-forward to my adolescence, and I quickly built the "overachiever" muscle. You know, the one that focuses on one goal after another? So, you never really stop, breathe, or acknowledge your success—you just move from one goal to the next, hoping the anxiety and pain deep inside will be smothered by the next success. I ran track and cross country, was editor of the high school newspaper, Homecoming Queen, was voted most popular in my senior class, and met my best friend, Angelica. Angelica saw me in a way no one else did—beyond the accomplishments, the accolades, and the image I projected. She showed me that I mattered just as I was, without needing to prove or achieve anything. Angelica became my "ride or die" best friend, the first person I could truly trust with my whole self. Thirty-five years later, she's still my greatest gift and my unwavering constant.

Despite these high school accomplishments, I often felt like I was holding my breath, waiting for the next disaster to strike. The lessons of my childhood—that nothing good lasts—were difficult to unlearn. Even as I was celebrated, I feared losing everything I had worked for, a fear that would carry over into adulthood.

I wish I could end my high school chapter on that note, but unfortunately, that was not the case. In December of my senior year, weeks before Christmas, two of my close friends were killed by a drunk driver. This was a tragic loss—one that shook the foundation of my adolescence and once again reinforced in me that "bad things happen, so tread carefully."

On to college. I completed my Associate's Degree. I thought I wanted to be a dentist, so I studied microbiology and cell science for one year. Proof that you can learn anything if you set your mind to it because I was definitely more of a writer than a scientist. I worked for a marketing company while in college, and they recruited me to run the business for them in San Diego. So, I packed my bags and moved from Florida to San Diego, where I knew absolutely no one. No degree yet, but I was an executive leading a substantial business. Reflecting back, this move was the first major test of my independence. It was terrifying to leave the familiar behind, but it also gave me the confidence to trust my instincts and rely on my resilience.

I closed that chapter and then opened two successful retail stores. I closed that chapter, went to work with a friend, Paula. I am eternally grateful for her belief in me and the opportunity she gave me to learn, grow, and lead her company. Together, we built a multinational fashion apparel company from $0 to $35 million. I started in the warehouse and got promoted to Operations Manager → VP of Operations → VP of Sales & Marketing → Executive Vice President, and finally President of the company. Oh, and I completed my Bachelor's Degree in Business Administration as the Executive Vice President. Sigh…Just keep running, and I won't slip through the cracks—that was my unspoken mantra.

Since my teens, I've been that person who never gave up, who constantly checked the boxes, took care of my body, and stayed late to get the job done. I basically just outworked everyone. But at 45, everything I'd been trying to outrun—my trauma, fears, and shame—finally caught up with me.

For years, I thought I was healing. I had endured a ton of personal growth and believed my trauma was a thing of the past. But it wasn't until I was 45 that my real healing began. Before that, I had been working long hours in challenging business environments, pouring my heart and soul into building founder-led businesses. But all that dedication took a toll on me mentally, physically, and emotionally. I was running towards the next goal and running away from old wounds.

I'll never forget the day it all came to a head. I was supposed to take my 12-year-old daughter to school, but I woke up and couldn't catch my breath. The anxiety was overwhelming. I paced back and forth on the pool deck, trying to get it together but couldn't. I had a full-on anxiety attack.

I called my husband and told him, "You've got to come home. I can't breathe." When he got home, he took our daughter to school, and then I just cried on his shoulder, realizing that I couldn't keep hiding behind being an overachiever. My daughter had no clue what was happening. I was so ashamed of the fact that I was breaking. The thought of being unable to take my daughter to school and not being the best version of myself for her was terrifying. I was slipping through the cracks and into the dark water. There was NO WAY I was going to let that happen.

That breakdown marked the beginning of a turning point. For the first time, I realized that success at the expense of my well-being wasn't truly success. It pushed me to reevaluate my priorities and confront the parts of my story I had buried.

For years, I buried myself in work, exercise, and always being "on," saying yes, even at the expense of my own health. I ignored the signs—like my back going out, grinding my teeth, and stomach issues—and focused on fixing the symptoms rather than addressing the root cause. That's where my healing journey began—at 45.

I met with a Life Coach weekly for a year, and for the first time, I understood why I was who I was and why I saw the world the way I did. It was so logical, and I didn't even have to relive every dark part of life to feel better about who I was. I just had to understand the "why."

My Life Coach was life changing. There were two pivotal and transformational moments. The first was a visual showing circles inside circles. She explained to me that I let everyone into my innermost circle—the most intimate, private parts of my story and my life. She explained that people should earn their way to that level of trust, even if they're family, which made so much sense to me. I lived my life pleasing people to survive, being whatever they needed me to be to feel accepted. I lost myself in the process and felt disappointed when they took advantage of my willingness to be raw and open. Makes sense, makes perfect sense. That tool was life changing. Let the boundary setting, without fear of disappointing people, begin.

The second pivotal moment was the "belief window." She explained that our life experiences, especially as children, make up what's called a "belief window." We see the world through this window. My belief window at the time was filled with Death, Abuse, Alcoholism, Fear, and Neglect. That explained my fear and anxiety. I was the person who crossed the street and imagined the worst-case scenario. I did this often. Once I understood this concept, I stopped judging myself for my thoughts and instead started to understand them, which was the catalyst for building new beliefs, healing, and breathing.

These breakthroughs didn't just help me personally; they reshaped how I approached leadership and relationships. The lessons I learned about trust and beliefs became tools I applied not only in my family life but also in my work, helping others overcome their own limiting beliefs.

I went on to get my Life Coaching Certification because why not? Yes, the overachiever muscle was still in full force. Seriously, though, I have transformed my life, so why not become an expert and help others? It's been a nice tool to have in my professional toolkit—one that differentiates me and, more importantly, moves mountains with clients.

That's the condensed version of my story, but it won't be my daughter's story. When I became a mother, I swore I'd give her the life I never had. I was 33 when I gave birth to my daughter. The best day of my life. I looked at her and knew I was born for this. I have a picture right after she was born, and she's looking at me as though we've known each other for a lifetime. I named her Shay Katherine Stacey. Katherine was my mom's name. So, here comes the next generation. I knew that I had to get this right.

I continued working and, of course, experienced the normal mom's guilt. I made up for it by always prioritizing her and keeping her at the center of my life. It's crazy because I had no manual for how to be a good mom. I often joke with friends that I was raised by wolves. I genuinely believe that. I was cleaning toilets to make money in my tweens. I don't remember having a childhood. To survive, I had to be an adult and take care of myself mentally and physically.

I told myself, *this will not be the story my daughter tells.* I will break this cycle. I will be the mother I wish I had. She will have the life I wish I had. She will feel heard and seen and know that she matters in this world.

My belief window: Death, Abuse, Alcoholism, Fear, Neglect.

Her belief window: Love, Fearlessness, Light, Happiness, Endless Possibilities.

She will not fear "slipping through the cracks." She will run on the pier and swim in the dark water—with excitement and without fear—and meet her God-given potential. That's how I'll break the generational patterns and crack the rich code.

I read all of the parenting books—I mean all of them, from letting your child cry themselves to sleep to when to introduce solid foods. I was a student of parenting. Then something strange happened—I decided that I would just trust my instincts. My life has shown me what I don't want, so why not use that as a blueprint to create something better? Yes, that's the trick.

As a baby, when my daughter cried, I held her. I held her until she was soothed. She was just a baby, not a manipulative, scheming human. Why would she cry if she didn't have a reason? And guess what? She cried less because she trusted me. She trusted that I would be there if she needed me, so she cried when she truly needed me. That was the first trust-building exercise that built the considerable muscle she has now. She trusts me and she trusts herself.

I remember being at her 2-year-old pediatrician appointment. I loved our pediatrician. He was so gentle and made the experience fun and positive. I'll never forget him talking about the "terrible twos" and saying just to be patient. Two-year-olds want to try things like fastening their seatbelts and opening doors. *Give yourself time so they can do those things, and I promise the terrible twos won't be so terrible,* he said. He was right. Such a simple concept and made so much sense. This wasn't in any of my parenting books, but I give this advice to every parent at that stage. It's priceless.

And then there's the tweens. They're no longer little people you dress and feed. They now have a point of view on what they wear and who their friends are. All of their friends' parents start to text you about their concerns and "what would you do" questions. Again, I went with my instincts. I was the parent who let my daughter choose her clothes, even if they didn't match. I mean, what's the harm in that? My take was, *She'll eventually figure it out,* and *Lose the battles, win the war.* Parents would come to me for advice, and I was confident in my parenting skills. I felt guided by the "what did I need at that age" compass, which served me well.

As my daughter grew up, I found many parallels between leading companies and parenting. Leading people was one of them. After having my daughter, I looked across the desk and imagined those I led as my sons or daughters. I'd structure my communication around feedback to map how I would want someone to speak with my daughter. This shifted my leadership style. I looked at each and every person I led as an opportunity to ensure they felt seen and heard and knew that they mattered to the business. This was a pivotal moment for me in my career.

Oh, and that belief window? I also leverage that tool in business. Business is about people, and people bring their "belief windows" to work. Sometimes, those windows include limiting beliefs that hold people and companies back from meeting their potential. That tool comes in handy and separates me from most leaders.

I also learned to listen—really listen—to those I led. When you create space for people to share their fears and dreams, you can help them rewrite their belief windows, just as I rewrote mine. This approach transformed not just my teams but also the culture of the companies I've been a part of.

I've built companies from the ground up and turned around underperforming companies. I've taken the same approach professionally as I have personally—learning from each experience and knowing what *not* to do has been my secret weapon. Trusting myself and building trust with others.

Now, my daughter is in her freshman year of college at Southern Nazarene University in Bethany, Oklahoma. She plays soccer and studies Business & Marketing. I look back at my 18 years with her and wonder where all the time went. People tell you it flies by, and they are right. You blink, and they're grown up. They still need you, but it's different now. She has a vision for her life. It may change, but for now, it's her vision. You realize that they no longer need you in the same way. They're in your life, but it's just so different now.

As I reflect on everything, I realize that breaking the cycle wasn't just about parenting differently or achieving success—it was about choosing a path of courage over fear, healing over avoidance, and authenticity over perfection. It's about showing my daughter and others that life's cracks don't have to define us; they can be the spaces where light gets in and helps us grow.

Today, I focus on helping others discover their own version of healing and resilience. Whether through my work with entrepreneurs, coaching clients, or sharing my story, my mission is clear: to empower people to rewrite their belief windows and embrace the possibilities ahead. I believe we all have the power to meet our God-given potential, no matter how deep the cracks or how dark the water may seem.

Cracking the rich code isn't about financial wealth alone—it's about breaking through the barriers that hold us back, rewriting the stories we've been told, and creating a life filled with purpose, love, and light. It's about living fearlessly, embracing every lesson, and building a legacy of healing and empowerment. At 52, I can confidently say I've cracked the code. Now, it's my turn to help others do the same.

***

To contact Kelly:

YouTube | https://www.youtube.com/@Kelly_Stacey

Podcast | https://podcasts.apple.com/us/podcast/conquer-your-constraints/id1762896977

Instagram | https://www.instagram.com/workwithkellystacey

Skool Community | https://www.skool.com/start-up-activator-3186

Website | https://workwithkellystacey.com/

Email | kelly@kellystaceyconsulting.com

Adam DeVito

Adam is a strategist, social impact entrepreneur and top coach and advisor to some of the world's most influential leaders. He has spearheaded large-scale strategy and innovation for many Fortune 500 and entrepreneurial companies, generating over $5 billion in incremental revenue.

In his mid-20s, Adam led cross-functional innovation at the world's largest food company. Along the way, he created the most successful new brand in Kraft's history.

As Managing Partner of Sterling Rice Group, Adam has led dozens of depth research, strategy, and large innovation initiatives across sectors. He has explored the nature of leadership, technology and change and has a passion for long-range scenario planning, sustainability and regeneration and human health behavioral models.

Adam launched an incubator focused on human play, catalyzing purpose-driven ventures like SuperBetter and Monj Inc., a digital health company which he co-founded to help people heal from lifestyle chronic illness through sustained lifestyle behavior change. Monj promotes the joy of food and emotional wellbeing —fostering deeper human connections.

Beginning at age 14, Adam apprenticed in world-renowned restaurants, then opened two culinary schools for professional chefs, and co-authored 12 highly successful books on healthy cooking.

Over the decades, Adam has worked with hundreds of C-suite leaders, fascinated by those who ignite inspiration, commitment and devotion – versus those who struggle to gain momentum. His passion lies at the intersection of leadership, transformation, and human potential.

The Inspired Leader:
The Inner Path to Growth & Success

By Adam DeVito

The Times, They Are a-Changin'

In the opening verses of Dylan's iconic 1964 song, we're urged:

"Come gather 'round people wherever you roam and admit that the waters around you have grown... If your time to you is worth savin', you better start swimmin' or you'll sink like a stone, for the times, they are a-changin'."

This anthem emerged in a time of upheaval—not unlike today. It also marked the dawn of the technological revolution. Moore's Law, the 1965 prediction that microchip capacity would double every two years, has proven to be correct and driven unimaginable change.

We are living through one of the most dynamic eras in human history. The pace of change is reshaping how we interact, adapt, and lead. AI and technology are enabling solutions at an unprecedented scale, mirroring human ingenuity and altering how we see ourselves and our place in the world. They touch every aspect of life.

In human *health*, we have real-time data, sharper diagnostics and even the ability to work on diseases before they appear. On a *social* level, technology fuels social movements and opens doors to personal growth and education like never before. In *business*, it boosts efficiency, expands global reach and helps us anticipate customer needs with personalized solutions. And AI will transform how we work entirely.

The Problem: Humans Weren't Built for This

Here's the challenge—Our evolutionary wiring isn't designed to keep pace with today's speed and scale. Our brains evolved for *gradual* adaptation as well as for connection, **not** exponential acceleration and much greater societal polarization. In fact, *Martec's*

Law tells us that our adaptation lags further behind every year, compounding our stress and cognitive overload.

Markets that once felt stable are shifting under our feet. Early-stage companies, freer to experiment, are disrupting almost all industries, often rapidly overtaking legacy players. Household names vanish while entire sectors reemerge in new forms. **We're living in an era of relentless disruption.** Staying agile amid distributed teams, endless data, and evolving tools feels like drinking from a firehose while juggling flaming bowling pins.

The toll is real: Leaders are frazzled by performance pressures and are disconnected from joy.

The numbers back it up:

- **80% of U.S. employees** seek help for work-related stress (*Haiilo, 2024*).
- **85% feel disengaged**, fueling turnover and lower productivity (*Gallup, 2020*).

When the ground keeps shifting faster and faster, leaders risk becoming reactive, overwhelmed, and cut off from themselves and others. Like frogs in a slowly boiling pot, it can be hard to see how unsustainable this all is.

A Wake-Up Call to the Self

How do we meet this challenge? By **reimagining leadership** from the inside out. What if we led with less force and more flow? What if teams were united by a **deeper shared purpose**?

The answer isn't more doing; it's deeper being – quieting the noise to hear the real signals, shifting from control to trust, and creating space for vision amid performance pressures. As Viktor Frankl famously reminds us:

"Between stimulus and response, there is a space... in our response lies our freedom."

If we cultivate new "superpowers" of self-leadership, all the data, along with my firsthand experience as an executive coach – shows that we can thrive in ways we've never imagined. The path forward is a *deliberate turn toward self-awareness*, where outward achievement harmonizes with inward reflection.

Shaping Time Through Self-Awareness

Time is our most precious currency—entirely non-renewable. And time doesn't just pass; we **live** each moment of it, whether actively or passively. Over a 70-year period, allowing for 8 hours for sleep, we have 24,528,000 awake moments. A universal experience I hear in my work with C-suite leaders from all sectors is a sense of racing against time … a near constant struggle to balance time deep in work with time for loved ones and self-care. In fact, we are often much more concerned about letting down a boss or co-worker than a loved one. While we may not be able to manufacture more time as we move from one thing to the next, we do have the opportunity to till our soil and **cultivate caring connections**.

This is the gateway to making our moments feel **full** and **expansive** versus scarce and distracted. And it's a form of honoring ourselves and others in our lives.

Trust Over Control: The Leadership Paradox

The more we try to control everything, the more we push *against* time rather than flowing. And the more we exhibit authority, the less influence we have. Self-aware leaders focus on what they can influence while building **trust**, igniting autonomy in others, and fostering collaboration—the raw ingredients for a regenerative culture.

It's important to recognize that despite the world's chaos and power shifts, we are in an era of **co-destiny**—where our choices ripple through teams and organizations. Uncertainty is real! But when leaders quiet the noise leading from the inside out, they become an anchor in the storm, enabling thoughtful, constructive responses over impulsive reactions—which further builds trust!

The Energy of Influence

Neuroscience, quantum physics and leadership psychology show that our thoughts, emotions and attention create an energetic frequency that directly affects others. Fear-based leadership – ***Low-Frequency*** energy driven by stress, control, and scarcity – leads to micromanagement, distrust, and decision paralysis that stifles creativity. The first shift moves into a ***Neutral Zone***, where awareness and **curiosity** spark coherence, learning, and collaboration. From there, some leaders reach ***High-Frequency*** states—characterized by flow, trust, and visionary action that uplift systems, drive innovation, and foster self-organizing teams.

This isn't just theory—it adds fresh layers to our leadership model, where awareness, attention, and high-frequency energy fuel transformation. Deep self-awareness and quality attention make us magnetic. When attuned to ourselves and others, we radiate an energy that attracts. Seriously … who doesn't want to be the kind of leader people actually want to follow?

But oh, the Challenges of the Mind!

Our minds are incredibly crowded—up to 60,000 thoughts per day, 90% of which are repetitive and 80% are negative. Research shows that multitasking is really just rapid-task-switching, further dividing our attention and energy while increasing stress and diminishing performance.

Chronic stress fuels "rumination loops," and fixations, while the dopamine-driven design of digital platforms traps us in endless cycles of self-monitoring, comparison, and social validation—a trend further amplified by FOPO (Fear of Other People's Opinions) compared to pre-internet times.

I see these patterns even in the highest-achieving leaders. They report feeling exhausted, frazzled, and overloaded, often accompanied by self-doubt and a harsh critic (inner and outer). When you show up to a meeting feeling irritable, distracted or in a thought loop, it sets a negative tone for everyone!

Here's A New Equation for Success

Attention + Alignment + Collective Purpose = Flourishing

- **Attention**: Pause and attune more to each moment with curiosity and awareness.

- **Alignment:** Integrating inner values and actions with agreements, practices and the collective purpose of the team, thereby enabling greater autonomy and connection.

- **Collective Purpose**: Being in service of something greater and more meaningful than a paycheck—a North Star, unlocking inspiration and a regenerative culture that replenishes itself.

- **Flourishing**: Leading with purpose, alignment, and sustained impact. Navigating uncertainty with greater clarity, inspiring through authenticity, and balancing ambition with well-being.. Flourishing leaders don't just chase outcomes; they cultivate environments where they and others thrive, where challenge fuels a growth mindset, and where fulfillment is found in both the journey and the destination.

So, How to Get Started?

Maybe you're now curious but you're still thinking, *I don't have time for personal discovery.* Well, in today's swirling tides, the ancient call to *know thyself* has never been more urgent.

And there's good news—Wisdom isn't about having *all* the answers, and you don't need to climb a mountaintop. It's about noticing when you veer off course and correcting yourself sooner. It's about remembering *why* you're on this journey in the first place. The first mountain to climb is within our own minds!

Let's demystify these foundational "secrets" and make them tangible—because the truth is, it's easier than you think.

1. Attention - The Gift of Mastering Your Focus

To pay attention means we care, which means we really love. Attention is the most basic form of love. By paying attention, we allow ourselves to be touched by life, and our hearts naturally become more open and engaged. — **Krishnamurti**

We start with attention because it's where we always start, whether we are tuned in or not. While many books detail the power of presence, here we'll briefly define *quality of attention* and consider what gets in the way for most of us. Then I'd like to offer some simple practices.

Defining Quality Attention

Quality attention is characterized by a **deliberate focus** on the present, whether directed toward a task, a person, or one's own internal experiences. The benefits are endless and include: enhanced performance; greater ability to read & respond to markets and to innovate; improved relationships & deeper connections; greater personal fulfillment & sense of accomplishment.

In contrast, passive attention often involves activities that require minimal cognitive effort (such as scrolling through social media posts) leading to a state of distraction or mental disengagement.

Key Attributes of Quality Attention

A. **Self-Awareness**: It all starts by recognizing our own thoughts, emotions, and energy, and understanding how they drive attention and engagement. This can also be called mindfulness, and it's the gateway to self-leadership.

B. **Intentionality**: Purposefully directing attention rather than letting it be hijacked by external distractions, biases or judgements based on past performance.

C. **Attunement**: The ability of leaders to sense and respond to the team's emotions and needs—it's about being present and being able to read subtle cues that build trust and collaboration.

Unpacking Stress

Stress is the most universal symptom of our time. It's like a fever **hijacking our attention**. Stress is *friction between demands and capacity,* pulling the mind, body and spirit out of alignment. It also emerges from internal conflict—*opposing thoughts* that burn fuel but go nowhere.

Three in four U.S. adults experienced stress-related health impacts within the last month (APA) while **43% feel more anxious** than last year (2024 survey). And we know that chronic stress is hard on our heart categorically leading to poor health outcomes!

The Foot on the Gas & Brake

Stress is like having one foot on the gas and one on the brake:

Gas = Ambition, drive, desire to make things happen.

Brake = Doubt, fear, overthinking, limiting beliefs.

Underneath it all? Old conditioning, unchecked stories, and resistance. Stress isn't just about what's happening—it's about the *stories we tell ourselves about what's happening.*

Leaking Energy

Resistance, in all of its forms, burns energy—whether it's grasping, clinging, or emotional friction (feelings of anger, fear, frustration, holding grievances). I call this leaking energy. Instead of seeing reality **as it is**, we get caught in the current of our stories and fixations, creating stress and wearing us down.

So, how do We Elevate Our Attention & Energy?

The place to begin is to recognize we are not our thoughts, and we are not the mind. We are *awareness* moving within the mind! See if you can sit with that for a few minutes with your eyes closed to begin to experience it. I am going to share a metaphor that is quite literally true: *Vision* emerges from a deeper awareness, thereby seeing things *clearly*. The more clearly we see things, the better we navigate obstacles, adapt to change and envision possible futures. Start by:

- **Recognizing the Resistance** – Listen to the self-talk. What **story** are you telling myself that is limiting you or creating resistance? Is it true?
- **Easing Up on the Brake** – Accept the moment **as it is**, not how you think it **should** be.
- **Adjusting Dynamically** – Flow beats force. If you're pushing too hard or fast, pause and realign. If you're feeling fear or trepidation, get in touch with that.
- **Owning Your Focus** – Where focus goes, energy flows. Choose wisely.

Think of awareness like a **ball of light**—direct it and energy follows. Stress then becomes an invitation to wake up, shift, and realign. Try smiling and say: "Nice try, foot on the brake. I see you. But I'm taking my foot off now."

Attention Practices:

- **Activate Self-Awareness** - Spend 5 minutes each morning and 2-3 minutes between meetings to breathe and compassionately notice your feelings, sensations, and recurring thoughts. This builds awareness and aligns you with your values.

- **Protect your Time** - Set clear boundaries, schedule deep work sessions, and prioritize good nutrition and sleep. Self-care is essential.

- **Propel Trust** – If self-leadership is the engine, trust is the fuel—the foundation of psychological safety and high-performing teams. It lowers stress (cortisol) and boosts connection (oxytocin), creating healthier, happier teams. Paired with purpose, it's a force multiplier.

Have the team sit in a circle to share a brief story of challenge or growth, followed by rounds of appreciative feedback where teammates share insights or relate their experiences. This builds trust through vulnerability and empathy.

- **Develop Attuned Listening to Build Empathy** - Attuned listening means fully engaging with another's words, tone, and body language to uncover deeper emotions and intentions. Research shows non-verbal cues significantly outweigh words.

Pair up with a colleague, assigning roles as sharer and receiver. The sharer tells a personal story while the receiver practices attuned listening—capturing key non-verbal cues, not just repeating words. Rotate roles so everyone experiences both perspectives.

2. Creating Alignment

"Follow effective action with quiet reflection. From the quiet reflection will come even more effective action." — Peter Drucker

It Starts with Internal Alignment:

The flow of demands in today's organizations is overwhelming, with the constant push for more, faster. In highly competitive environments, companies often focus on defending market share, driving incremental improvements, or boosting productivity, leaving little space for transformational innovation. As a result, prioritizing and distinguishing what truly matters becomes increasingly difficult. Like attention, alignment starts within. Leaders who are out of sync with their values create friction and confusion. The most effective leaders know alignment is a dynamic process that requires continuous evaluation and careful consideration of others. This approach fosters clarity and trust, opening the door to a more collaborative culture.

... Leading to Organizational Alignment:

When leaders loosen control and team members are empowered to contribute and act in service of the whole, a sense of collective ownership emerges. The hierarchical divide fades as responsibilities are shared, fostering cohesive decision-making and unified goals.

... Increasing the Likelihood of Flourishing:

When individuals and teams are empowered and aligned, organizations unleash a large network of **co-leaders** that make them smarter and more responsive in fast-changing markets. This increases the likelihood that the organization will navigate challenges successfully and emerge stronger.

Here are 5 steps to take to drive business alignment:

1. **Clarify Roles & Values** - Ensure each team member knows their unique strengths and why they matter.

2. **Identify Energy Drains & Blocks** - Spot and clear obstacles—misalignment, outdated processes, or unspoken tensions.

3. **Foster Open Dialogue** - Check in regularly and engage in honest, two-way communication where everyone feels safe to share and innovate.

4. **Adapt in Real-Time** - Encourage quick, micro-adjustments—small shifts to keep the team agile and on course before issues escalate. Don't forget to look to the future!

5. **Cultivate Ownership:** - Create an environment of psychological safety and empowered ownership that leads teams to work together, co-create and align naturally.

Alignment Practices:

1. **Uncover your Superpowers:** Identify each team member's unique strengths by visiting VIAcharacter.org for a free, scientifically validated strengths survey. Then, work with a coach to activate them!

2. **Powering Up Reflection** – Philosopher and educator John Dewey said, *We do not learn from experience… we learn from reflecting on experience."* A sense of spaciousness calms the nervous system acting as a reset button. How do we create spaciousness? Create it by asking each person: "Reflect on one key insight gained today, and how could you apply it moving forward?" Then, encourage them to jot down and share their thoughts.

3. **Kick-Off Scenario Planning** – Enhance strategic thinking by engaging in facilitated simulation games that imagine possible future challenges and crisis scenarios. Then consider how the company might respond and what actions can avert negative outcomes.

3. The Power of Collective Purpose

Collective purpose is an organization's secret weapon—uniting teams and organizations in service of something more meaningful than just financial performance. Leading with Purpose creates the glue to pull together rather than pushing against one another. Whether a large and small organization, Purpose can create a huge competitive advantage when combined with *attention* and *alignment.*

Unlocking collective purpose isn't just a noble cause; it's highly strategic:

- A mission statement tells the world *what* you do.
- A vision statement paints a picture of *where* you're headed.

- A collective purpose explains *why* you exist. Much more than words on a wall, it's a "north star" that rallies the organization and considers the wellbeing of a broader range of stakeholders, starting with the employees themselves.

Goals vs. Purpose: The Empty Chase vs. The Energizing Pursuit

Organizations have long chased KPIs and revenue targets, believing what gets measured gets managed. And sure, tracking progress matters. But when goals drive only financial performance, they often fail to ignite the human spirit, leaving people exhausted, disengaged, and quietly resentful.

Here's the truth:

- You hit the numbers, and what happens? It can be a thrill for a moment but you're immediately *onto the next target*. No real sense of fulfillment. No deeper connection.
- You miss the numbers, *pressure* and *stress* mount.

In either case, there's no lasting motivation.

As leaders, it's time to break free from constant pressure and reconnect with passion. Instead of asking what we do and where we're headed, we must ask *why we matter* and *who we are*—even when no one's watching. This shift unlocks a deeper source of meaning, fueling sustained inspiration for the team.

Leading with Purpose Isn't a Fad—It's a Movement. Here's Why:

- **Innovation**: Purpose-driven organizations out-innovate their competitors by 30% (Deloitte)
- **Engagement:** 73% of employees in purpose-led companies are engaged—compared to just 23% in others. (Inc.)
- **Retention:** Purpose-driven companies experience 40% higher retention. (Deloitte)

- **Financial Performance**: And they grow three times faster than competitors and gain greater market share. (Deloitte)

The Shift: From Individual Success to Collective Strength

Just as AI thrives on intelligence from the "collective", purpose-driven companies harness diverse thought and mission alignment to create something greater than the sum of their parts. The focus shifts from individual and divisional success to the success of the whole.

The Result? Antifragile Organizations That Thrive in Change

Purpose-driven companies not only survive disruption—they grow stronger because of it. They cultivate:

Trust – Engaged, self-led employees.

Resilience – Setbacks may slow momentum but don't break it.

Loyalty – Customers and other stakeholders become passionate brand advocates.

I've seen the power of Purpose firsthand, working with leaders of dozens of companies—from early-stage software that scaled into multi-billion-dollar businesses, to packaged goods companies that outgrew their competitors by a large margin.

Purpose Is an Operating System, Not a Slogan

Companies that lead with purpose embed it into every decision, not just marketing. It is visible in leadership actions, employee behavior, and customer experience.

Purpose Practices:

This rich area can most effectively be pursued with the guidance of a coach. Here are some ideas to start:

> **1. Personal Purpose Challenge** - Craft a single sentence-long statement that captures your unique contribution, passion, and vision at your highest state. Start by writing key words, string together into a present tense statement and refine until it feels inspirational and authentic to you.

2. Annual Purpose Reset – Dedicate time each year outside of the office for leaders to tune in, reflect and recommit to collective purpose.

3. Investigate & Activate Self-Determination. – Explore Dr. Edward Deci's model of Self-Determination Theory https://selfdeterminationtheory.org/theory/. On the same topic, add Daniel Pink's book *Drive* to your reading list.

In Closing…

Organizations large and small **flourish** and create sustained success when leaders at all levels internalize purpose with greater self-awareness and deep team alignment. This creates more resilient and inspired workplace cultures able to navigate uncertainty with clarity, authenticity, and balanced ambition … where challenges spark reflection and growth, and where fulfillment is found in both the journey and destination. And I highly recommend bringing on a top coach (or two) to accelerate integration of these rich

I help clients activate the power within. Please reach out to engage any time!

***

To contact Adam:

adam@APD-coaching.com

https://www.linkedin.com/in/adam-devito-755b07/

Mobile: 720 839 5747

APD-Coaching: Coaching and advising top leaders and teams to navigate growth and outward achievement through greater empowerment & self-mastery

Isaac Garcia

Isaac Garcia is a transformation coach, leadership mentor, and Agile expert dedicated to helping high performers navigate change and uncertainty without losing sight of what truly matters. He believes resilience isn't just about endurance, it's about adapting, leading, and thriving.

Since embracing agile in 2015, Isaac has served as a Scrum Master, Agile Coach, and Transformation Coach, guiding organizations, teams, and individuals to achieve sustainable high performance through a balance of agility, resilience, and well-being. His coaching blends strategic execution with mental and emotional resilience, empowering leaders to scale their impact without burning out.

Isaac is a founding member of Coaching Agile Journeys, a virtual agile meetup that has interviewed over 60 world-class coaches and hosted numerous community events. His work extends beyond coaching—he actively fosters environments where continuous learning, adaptability, and intentional growth thrive.

Isaac provides coaching, speaking, and training for executives, entrepreneurs, and professionals seeking to build resilient leadership, drive meaningful change and create long-term success. His expertise in agility, leadership, and human performance equips individuals with the skills to excel under pressure, adapt to uncertainty, and turn challenges into opportunities.

Whether coaching organizations, mentoring professionals, or shaping the future of leadership, Isaac is committed to helping people lead with clarity, resilience, and impact—so they can not only succeed but truly thrive.

It's Just Not Working Anymore

By Isaac Garcia

You've done everything you were supposed to do. You checked the boxes: work hard, stay late, sacrifice sleep, and push yourself to the limit. And yet, instead of feeling like you are moving forward, you just feel exhausted. Instead of feeling successful, you feel stuck. Some days, you just look out the window and wonder if all this focus and work is even worth it.

Have you felt that? You're doing everything—hustling, showing up, giving it your all—to get ahead, win, and finally catch that break. Maybe you thought it would lead to the life you've been working so hard for or at least make you worthy of a moment's rest. But the results just aren't there.

You hit your deadlines and pushed through exhaustion, but you feel like you're running in place instead of breaking through. The results aren't matching the effort—and that's exhausting. You've heard the saying, "What got you here won't get you there." But what are you supposed to change when you're already doing your best?

Ever feel like George Banks from Mary Poppins, mindlessly singing, 'Grind, grind, grind at that grindstone'? Is that just the way it has to be?

Or maybe you are crushing it. You're achieving your goals and making things happen, but something still feels… off. That nagging question— "What's next?" or "Is this all there is?"—keeps creeping in.

Either way, let's take a moment. A quick reflection. A pause in the activity. A retrospective on your latest wins and losses. Maybe even a much-needed shift into a new gear.

But before we discuss resilience, take a moment to consider how you're feeling right now. Tired? Overwhelmed? Frustrated? Moving forward in a way that sustains you—rather than drains you—starts with two key elements: resilience and you.

Start With You

Before we dive into resilience, let's start with the most important part of the equation—you.

You are a unique, powerful human being with incredible capacity and adaptability. You don't need to measure yourself against anyone else. You are in a category of one. The key isn't comparison; it's understanding, leveraging, and growing to your full potential.

You are a critical part of any success that will happen in and through your life. For your sake and the world's sake, please don't leave your unique song unsung during this complex and changing time. Someone, somewhere, needs what only you can give.

Now, I want to offer some ideas that can directly impact your near- and long-term success. This isn't just about performance, it's an invitation to a healthier mental, physical, and social reality.

Is Everything You've Been Told About Resilience Wrong?

Resilience is often misunderstood.

For years, we've been sold the idea that resilience means pushing through, staying tough, and enduring no matter the cost. "Keep grinding." "Push harder." "No pain, no gain." Sound familiar?

This mindset might help in the short term, but over time, it leads to exhaustion, frustration, and burnout (trust me, I know). It was built for a world with fewer distractions—when work had a clear beginning and end, and rest was a natural part of life.

But work and life blur together today and pushing harder isn't the answer. True resilience—Healthy Resilience—isn't about endless endurance. It's about adaptability, energy management, and sustainable growth amid an increasingly complex and evolving world.

So, what does Healthy Resilience actually look like? First, it's self-awareness—knowing when to push, when to pause, when to pivot. It's agility—staying open to change instead of fighting it. And maybe most importantly? It's restoration—learning to recover and recharge so you don't run into the ground.

Seriously. Rest.

When our physical, mental, and emotional lifestyle is unhealthy, we sacrifice ourselves in the name of progress. When it's healthy, we become stronger, more effective, and capable of thriving—even in the face of uncertainty. The incredible reality is that healthy sustainability is the only way to create lasting and fulfilling progress.

Healthy resilience isn't just about surviving the storm. It's about learning how to dance in the rain.

The Three Core Shifts to Build Healthy Resilience

To cultivate Healthy Resilience, you need to rethink how you approach challenges. Here are three initial mindset resets to get you started.

Shift #1: From Endurance to Adaptability

Resilience isn't about how much you can endure or how hard you can push. The most successful leaders don't just work harder, they work smarter, knowing when to pivot, adjust, and double down.

Think about trees in a storm. The ones that survive aren't the stiff, rigid ones that resist the wind. They're the flexible ones that bend and sway, adjusting to the force of the storm instead of fighting against it.

True resilience is about responding to change, not resisting it. It involves embracing challenges with a growth mindset (see Carol Dweck's 'The Power of Yet') rather than resisting change.

Takeaway: Instead of asking, "How can I push through this?" start asking, "How can I adjust and respond more effectively?"

Reframing: "The obstacle is the way." That challenge in front of you isn't a roadblock, it's an opportunity to grow wiser and stronger.

Shift #2: From Suppression to Emotional Mastery

Ignoring emotions doesn't make you stronger, it makes you weaker.

Think of emotions like a car's dashboard lights. If the check engine light comes on, don't cover it with a sticker and pretend it's fine. You take action. The same applies to stress, exhaustion, or frustration—they're signals that something needs attention.

Takeaway: Instead of suppressing emotions, practice checking in with yourself. Ask, "What is this feeling telling me?"

Reframing: Every emotion has a root and a story. Take time to reflect on your last three strong emotional responses and ask if they served you well or should be adapted—it's time well invested.

Shift #3: From Burnout to Sustainable Growth

Burnout sneaks in disguised as drive, but it can quickly set fire to your emotional and physical well-being. You tell yourself you're just working harder for a season—until exhaustion, frustration, and overwhelm become the norm. Ask yourself right now, when was the last time you felt truly rested? And here's the sobering truth—burnout doesn't just hurt you; it hurts those closest to you; it hurts your results, your reputation, and your ability to lead effectively.

Elite athletes don't train at 100% intensity every day. They cycle through training and recovery. Healthy resilience follows the same principle—you can't perform at your best if you don't also build in recovery.

Takeaway: Instead of asking, "How much more can I handle?" start asking, "How can I set myself up for long-term success?"

Reframing: Keep a soft focus—see the bigger picture.

Applying Healthy Resilience in Daily Life

Resilience isn't built in a single moment. It's built in small, daily choices (see the book Atomic Habits by James Clear, Tiny Habits by BJ Fogg, or Elastic Habits by Stephen Guise). These choices build into a pattern of how you respond to stress, recover, and show up when things don't go as planned.

Right now, I want you to take a moment and reflect.

- Where in your life are you pushing through when you could be growing?
- Where are your gears grinding and causing you discomfort?
- Where do you know you need a change?

Maybe it's in your work—where you feel stuck in an endless string of work that doesn't really energize you. Maybe it's in your personal life—where you keep telling yourself you'll "get through it" or "fix it later" but never really feel at ease. Or maybe it's in your leadership—where you feel the pressure to have all the answers, be right all the time, always be strong, and never show weakness, but inside, you're exhausted.

The good news? You don't have to overhaul everything, everywhere, all at once to start building Healthy Resilience. Small shifts—one decision at a time—will make the difference.

The Micro-Adjustment Approach

Big changes feel overwhelming—like staring up at a mountain, unsure where to start. But here's the secret—sustainable success isn't about pushing harder; it's about knowing when to step back, strategize, and then move forward smarter. Instead of trying to transform your entire approach overnight, start with micro-adjustments, small but intentional shifts in your daily life.

Start right now. Actually, do this right now.

- Take a deep breath.
- Name one thing aloud you are thankful for.
- Take another deep breath.
- Name one person aloud that you are thankful for.
- Take one more deep breath.
- Name one thing about yourself that you are thankful for.

Small changes. Small moments. Small investments, made regularly, lead to big returns.

Consider these other potential micro-adjustments this week:

#1 Pause & Assess Before Reacting

When you feel overwhelmed, take a deep breath. Instead of reacting immediately, ask:

- "What's really happening here?"
- "Am I pushing when I should be pivoting?"

- "What's within my control?"

Even five extra seconds of awareness before reacting can create clarity.

#2 Build Your Energy Reserves (Instead of Just Spending Them)

Every action you take is either adding to your energy reserves or draining them.

Check-in with yourself:

- What restores you? Is it a quick walk, a deep breath, music, journaling, or talking to a friend?
- Do one small thing each day that refuels you.
- Reframe: Instead of saying, "I don't have time to rest," ask, "How can I make recovery a normal part of my routine?"

#3 Embrace the Power of the "One Thing" Rule

Resilience isn't about doing everything. It's about focusing on one impactful thing at a time.

Each morning, ask:

- "What's the ONE thing I can do today that will create momentum?"
- At the end of the day, reflect: "What's one thing I learned today that will help me tomorrow?"

Your Resilience Reflection Challenge

Healthy resilience isn't about grand, dramatic changes. It's about consistent, intentional micro-adjustments.

Pause for a moment. Seriously. Before you move on, take a deep breath. Slow down. Close your eyes if you need to.

Now, grab a notebook or open your notes app. Answer these three questions…

- Where am I pushing through when I should be adapting?
- What's draining my energy, and what's refueling it?

- What's one small, healthy change I can make today?

Exercises like this aren't just for reflection. This is strategy. Top leaders invest time to analyze what's working and what's not. I strongly encourage you to actually do this. Answer these three questions, as well as any others related to your resilience that you might be avoiding because you don't like their answers.

No judgment on yourself if you aren't where you want to be today. Pause. Breathe. Give yourself permission to grow through these challenges, not just survive it.

Growing Up With Your Resilience

Because resilience isn't about getting through life; it's about thriving in it.

But you already knew that. You are already more resilient than you think.

Every challenge you've faced, every obstacle you've navigated, and every moment you've chosen to adapt and keep going has shaped you into who you are today. And the best part? Resilience isn't just something you have—it's something you build.

The small choices you make each day—how you respond to stress, restore your energy, and embrace change—are the foundation of Healthy Resilience. It's not about enduring more. It's about adapting, growing, and thriving.

Consider for a moment the most resilient among us—children. They fall, get back up, and keep learning. The best leaders? They never stop learning, adjusting, and evolving. As they learn and grow in the first 10 years of their lives, they are constantly adapting, learning, questioning, changing, growing, and thriving with the right guidance, support, and environment.

- Where can you change your environment?
- Where can you reach out to ask for guidance?
- Who can you turn to for support?

One More Big Idea for Living in Healthy Resilience

Healthy resilience isn't just about responding to challenges, it's about proactively designing a life that supports your well-being. That means:

- Shaping Your Environment for Resilience.
    - The spaces, people, and habits in your life either support your resilience or drain it.
    - Take inventory of your physical, mental, and emotional environment and make small adjustments to create conditions where resilience thrives.
- Focusing on Rhythms, Not Just Habits.
    - Healthy resilience is a cycle, not a checklist.
    - Instead of obsessing over rigid productivity systems, think about energy rhythms—when you work best, when you recharge best, and how you can align your routines with those natural patterns.
- Redefining What Strength Looks Like.
    - Strength isn't about pushing harder, it's about knowing when to pivot, when to pause, and when to persist.
    - Your ability to adjust with wisdom rather than push with force is a real strength.

Look, I know what you're thinking— 'I don't have time to slow down to make all these changes.' I used to think that, too. To be honest, I sometimes still feel that way. But here's the truth: The top 1% of performers don't just work hard; they rest strategically— because they know burnout wrecks your results. It limits your potential. It steals your joy.

Quick Recap: The 3 Most Important Takeaways from This Chapter

#1 Resilience isn't about endurance, it's about adaptability.

- The strongest leaders aren't the ones who push through at all costs.
- They're the ones who learn to adjust and move forward with agility.

#2 Your emotions are part of resilience, not a weakness.
- Ignoring emotions doesn't make you stronger—it makes you disconnected.
- Your emotions provide valuable data—listen to them.

#3 Sustainable growth beats burnout every time.
- Rest isn't a reward; it's part of the process.
- The best way to maintain long-term success is to manage your energy, not just your time.

Your Next Step: A Challenge for You

So here's my challenge for you: Pick one small shift from this chapter and apply it today.
- Maybe it's pausing before reacting to a stressful moment.
- Maybe it's choosing one thing to focus on instead of feeling overwhelmed.
- Maybe it's giving yourself permission to rest and recharge.

Whatever it is, start small. Small shifts lead to big changes. And great leaders, the ones who create lasting impact, don't wait for resilience to happen. They build it. They invest the time to learn to adapt, evolve, and lead with resilience. So, what's the first shift you'll make today?

And remember: Resilience isn't about getting through life. It's about thriving in it. And this is just the beginning—what you do next will shape your future. Build your resilience, lead with adaptability, and step into a stronger version of yourself.

Enjoy the journey, my friend.

If this message resonated, let's connect. I'm passionate about helping leaders build resilience, avoid burnout, and create lasting success. I'd love to hear your thoughts and continue the conversation.

***

To connect with Isaac:

Email: Isaac@agiletechcoach.com

Website: www.AgileTechCoach.com

LinkedIn: https://www.linkedin.com/in/isaacgarciapro/

Nathan Baws

The Dopamine-Driven Business Builder, Nathan Baws is a serial business builder, speaker, author who has launched and scaled 15+ businesses across multiple industries. He's appeared on Shark Tank Australia, holds a Guinness World Record for ice baths, and thrives on shaking up the business world with unconventional strategies.

At six years old, after one too many budget-friendly baked potatoes, Nathan launched his first business - selling paper planes - to upgrade from starch to steak. Since then, his hunger for business took off, and he has been building and scaling businesses ever since.

Game-Changing Business Wins

Health Industry Leader: Record-breaking supplement sales for Australia's 2 biggest vitamin brands for 8 consecutive years.

Business Growth Hacker: Scales businesses using his 9-step organic growth strategy.

Business Builder:

3 health stores, 8 naturopathic clinics & his own national vitamin supplement brand

Property investment & training across Australia, UK & USA

Founded Tommy Sugo - a 7-stream-revenue food brand

Founded Emersion Wellness - a global hotel weight-loss program

Co-Founded Business Profit Lab - unlimited business marketing services

Co-Founded Flare School - a global financial literacy program for kid

Board member / partner in multiple startups

The Dopamine-Driven Business Builder

By Nathan Baws

Growing a business to me is all about stacking every possible tool, trick and system in my favor to create an unfair, impossible-to-fail, business advantage. I've built 17 businesses in vastly different industries, some hugely profitable and others that have failed miserably! I have seen firsthand the difference between struggling businesses and those that scale fast comes down to 2 critical factors:

- **Business Growth Strategies** - Test, refine, and scale proven marketing, sales, and lead generation tactics daily.
- **Mindset, Health & Dopamine** - Fuel resilience and sustained energy for unstoppable growth tactic implementation for long-term success.

In this chapter, you'll get powerful, actionable strategies to drive rapid and sustained business growth. While instant success matters, staying strong for the long game is key.

I'll share the exact strategies, health tips, and mindset hacks I use with one singular goal - to help you achieve explosive business growth! Just as elite athletes optimize fitness and technique to win, business leaders must master mindset, energy, and execution of technique to dominate.

Business is a high-performance sport, and I believe long term success comes from mental resilience, peak health, and growth strategies. It's hard to implement growth strategies consistently without optimizing mindset. You can do it, but it's an uphill battle. You'll learn how to harness dopamine for motivation, scale with zero-cost strategies, and optimize your routine for peak performance.

Many entrepreneurs chase revenue alone but lack resilience when the going gets tough. I'm passionate about mastering business growth and wellness for long-term, high-performance success. If you're serious about building a thriving business without burnout, pushing through challenges, and having a blast along the way, this chapter is your blueprint.

In The Beginning, God Made Potatoes...

Growing up in Western Australia, my dinners were 90% potatoes - cheap, filling but endlessly repetitive. My fiercely independent mum (single parent) refused financial help unless it came in the exact size, shape, and flavor she ordered. By six, I'd had enough. I needed money to help mum upgrade from potatoes to the occasional steak.

Spending a week on my cousin's farm, I made a bold declaration: "By the end of this week, I will make money, so I never have to see another potato again!".

Plan #1: Make money... literally!

Armed with bottle caps and a permanent marker, we "made money" scribbling "20c" on each cap. Shockingly, they looked nothing like the coins in mum's purse. Plan crushed.

Plan #2: Start a Business

Next, we turned a 6-year-old's top skill into a business - making paper airplanes. Several problems prevented a lucrative outcome: no signage, no marketing, no customers. Three hours, two cars passing, zero sales - lessons learned!

- If people don't know what you're selling, they won't buy. Now, every business I run ensures clear communication.
- Go where the hungry crowd is. Selling roadside from an empty paddock would work...if cows could buy!
- Find demand or create it.
- Marketing matters more than the product. Establish how you can get more people buying.

At six, I wasn't quite snapping on the heels of Richard Branson's aviation empire, but those early lessons activated my passion for business.

Understanding the value of early financial education, I recently co-founded www.flareschool.com, a school-based real-world financial literacy course for kids. It's the head start I wish I had at six - one that could have accelerated my business journey.

So, master sales, customer acquisition and lead generation early in your business life or be prepared to eat a lot of potatoes.

LEAD GENERATION

Lead generation is the lifeline of business - without it, there's no sales, no revenue, and no business. With a steady flow of leads, you can make sales, crush cash flow issues, boost profits, and eliminate financial stress.

If you're not generating leads daily, you're gambling with your future. Growth isn't luck - it's strategy.

I target 100+ leads per business per day because, with a 1-3% industry standard conversion rate, volume is everything. You can tweak your offer and variables to boost conversion, but business is a numbers game - focus on lead generation, or you're out of the game.

Are You Too Busy to Grow?

Be honest - are you scaling your business, or just keeping busy? If lead generation and sales aren't your top priority, make them! Sales should always come first. Period! More revenue from more sales lets you delegate tasks, hire a team member and focus on scaling instead of survival.

The 3-Hour Bawsome Business Builder
Bawsome (adj.) – /ˈbɔː-səm/ (*BAW-sum*)

Exceedingly awesome in business. Bold strategies, fearless execution, and undeniable success. Bawsome is my shamelessly self-indulgent nod to my surname, Baws. If it sounds like 'boss,' why not make it a movement?

Example: "Landing three JV deals in a week? Now that's Bawsome!"

Imagine dedicating three hours a day, five days a week, for 50 weeks a year to business growth (yes, I gave you 2 weeks off a year, you're welcome!). That equates to 750 hours a year - or 94 full business days - focused purely on scaling sales and business growth.

With battle-tested lead generation strategies, what impact could this relentless growth focus have on your business performance?

Follow these 3 steps to scale the bejeezus out of your business:
- Prioritize lead generation daily - no excuses.
- Eliminate or delegate low-value, non-business growth tasks.
- Stay consistent - momentum compounds.

Outsource the work or devote the time needed daily for sales growth activities. Do it like your business depends on it...because it does!

The Bawsome 9 Business Growth Strategies

The following 9 powerful strategies help me fuel consistent growth, launch new ventures, and drive up to 25% annual gains. Use them daily and watch your business thrive!

- **Direct Outreach** - Send cold messages, emails, and DMs daily. Automation lets us generate leads while we sleep. Use all the tools available.

- **Follow-Ups** - Most sales happen in the follow-up. Get to "yes" quickly or automate the rest. Don't waste energy on the wrong prospects - nurture, move fast, and focus on the next deal.

- **Email Marketing** - Send valuable content, offers, and updates to your email list. Avoid the sales pitch fest, send benefit-rich emails of value to the recipient to boost email open rates.

- **Social Media** - I target competitors' followers on Instagram and Facebook with direct, automated cold messages and special offers - encouraging competitors' audience to switch to the good guys. Cheeky but effective. General posting when you only have a small following is a slow burn (aka a waste of time). I prefer fast, direct outreach that gets results!

- **Cold Calling / Video Messages** - Personalized AI video messages grab attention fast. We customize every video outreach with recipients' names & business details to boost engagement. Hit me up on www.nathanbaws.com to get the latest tools we use.

- **Search Engine Optimisation (SEO)** - SEO is a long-term lead generation powerhouse, ranking your website on page

1 of google. I love SEO - it rings the cash register while I sleep. My team produces 2-4 highly optimized articles daily, ranking my websites for thousands of search terms.

I've wasted far too much money on SEO companies, trusting their "long-term results" promise - only to realize they were overpriced and underperforming. With no technical knowledge, I hired my own in-house SEO team and learnt firsthand how to drive real business growth with SEO.

Many businesses pour significant money into SEO without knowing if their investment is actually paying off - they have no clue what their SEO company is really doing or how effective their work is until they have paid them for way too long.

So we created a **FREE SEO Work Audit** to expose what SEO providers are actually doing. It **reviews strategies, tracks SEO work, holds providers accountable, and ensures your SEO investments will lead to real growth**.

Want to know if your SEO company is delivering? **Get a free audit at** www.nathanbaws.com/seo-audit.

Stop guessing. Start tracking. Make SEO work!

- **Build Your Database**

At Tommy Sugo (www.tommysugo.com.au), we've built a huge customer database with customer names, phone numbers and emails - all ours to keep. Unlike social media, where you can be banned in seconds for wearing the wrong aftershave while posting, your database can never be taken away! Email & SMS marketing to your database is basically free and insanely powerful.

- **Paid Advertising (or Creative Thinking)**

I don't use paid advertising and here's why. It's because God made potatoes! Limited resources are always beneficial to pose the question "how can I achieve the same results or better for FREE?"

My upbringing forced me to think creatively, build skills, and find solutions that unlimited funding wouldn't have. Here are a few examples:

a) My First Real Business

At 19, while studying Naturopathy, I saw an opportunity with the college's iridology-eye-examination machines - expensive devices that few students used. I borrowed one for free, set up at a local market, and offered health checkups. While my friends made $40–$60 flipping burgers, I pulled in $200–$400 a day - all with zero investment and a bit of creativity.

b) Creative Real Estate Purchases Without Finance

After a 7-figure health shop exit, I joined my sister Rachel in London to grow our property portfolio - she built a property empire on a dime (check out her chapter!).

Then, the GFC hit. Banks froze lending. So we asked: "How do we scale without using our own limited capital or bank loans?"

We found an Australian creative financing system which allowed us to acquire properties without banks or personal funds. Three years later, we had built a profitable portfolio - proof that resourcefulness beats capital, and you don't need money to make money!

- **Joint Venture (JV) Partnerships**

I saved the best for last! JVs are my **#1 strategy** for fast**, zero-cost** business growth. They let you **scale without risk, build credibility, and tap into ready-to-buy customers** without spending a cent on ads.

It's easy - **team up with a non-competing business**, create a **mutually beneficial offer**, and **sell more together** than you ever could alone.

Keep it **simple and fast to execute.** I've used this exact formula to generate **tens of thousands of dollars in sales across multiple businesses** and here's how to do it:

a) Find the Right JV Partner

Team up with non-competing businesses that share your ideal customers. The right partner gives instant access to a hungry audience.

b) Craft an Irresistible Win-Win-Win Offer

Your JV must benefit 3 parties - your JV partner, their customer and you! Forget vague "brand awareness" goals - sales always come first! If your offer doesn't make people say, "OMG, I NEED this" make it better!

Bawsome Tip: Get suppliers to contribute to your marketing! I've secured thousands of dollars in supplier-backed contributions that boosted my sales and suppliers benefited. Cash, product, discounts - be creative in your requests!

c) Keep It Simple & Scalable

Your offer should be so good it sells itself but must never leave you out of pocket! Structure it so you can run it forever, scaling without limits. If it goes viral, you win big.

d) Nail the JV Deal Structure

Decide upfront on commissions, revenue shares, or value exchanges - keep it crystal clear. A simple one-page friendly agreement works. Overcomplicate it, and your JV will stall before it even starts.

e) Make It Effortless for Your Partner

Hand them pre-written emails, social media posts, and promo scripts so they don't have to lift a finger. The less work they do, the faster they say yes.

f) Leverage Their Audience

Tap into their email list, social media, stores, or events. Most will endorse you and share your offer to their audience.

g) Track, Optimize & Repeat

Use trackable links, promo codes, or automation to prove every sale. I automate receipts so JV partners instantly see every dollar they earn. More trust = more desire to do business with you.

h) Scale & Multiply

A successful JV should be repeated, multiplied, and expanded to more partners. Set it up as a repeated frequency e.g. every quarter and watch your revenue soar.

Joint ventures are the ultimate zero-cost growth hack. Perfect the process, rinse, and repeat for unlimited sales!

Here are some real-life examples I currently use to grow my businesses with JV Partnerships:

Nathan Baws & Business Profit Lab

At www.nathanbaws.com & www.businessprofitlab.com.au, James (my growth-centric business partner) and I create high-impact JVs with accountancy firms that make growth effortless.

It's a Win-Win-Win JV model.

WIN: Accountants strengthen client relationships effortlessly bringing them growth value.

WIN: Business owners gain real growth strategies.

WIN: We connect with our ideal clients.

Zero cost, massive impact, powerful JV's!

Tommy Sugo's Hassle-Free School Fundraising JV's

At www.tommysugo.com.au (home delivered meals), we've made fundraising effortless - no more time-consuming sausage sizzles/cookouts for parents! We ensure minimal work is required from our joint venture partners by providing them with prewritten emails and social media posts for their database, plus we take care of order forms, payments and delivery.

It's a Win-Win-Win JV model.

WIN: Parents love an easy, hassle-free way to support their school as both fundraiser organizers and fundraiser product purchasers.

WIN: Schools, clubs, and charities raise funds effortlessly - they simply share the fundraiser link and earn from every order.

WIN: Tommy Sugo gains exposure and sales to hundreds of new ideal customers.

Hotel & Weight Loss Joint Ventures

Through www.emersionwellness.com, we help hotels implement weight loss wellness programs with a Win-Win-Win JV model:

WIN: Hotels do what they do best - offer accommodation, food, and services. Weight loss guests stay 7-21 days, increasing hotel room, meal, and service revenue. Emersion Wellness increases hotel revenue at no cost to hotels - guests cover the fees.

WIN: Guests win by enjoying a flexible, tailored weight loss program in beautiful hotels.

WIN: Emersion Wellness delivers professional virtual weight loss programs, putting the backend of the program together. We win by partnering with top hotels & gaining access to massive customer exposure.

Zero risk, huge upside, easy execution - a game-changer in hotel wellness and a JV that delivers massive value for all involved!

As sales guru Brian Tracy (featured in this book's foreword) says, "Make your offer so good, saying no isn't an option."

Bawsome Tip: A super juicy JV partner offer will open well-oiled doors, spark interest and leads to a fast "YES" from JV partners. Get your foot in the door easily by offering massive value - otherwise, you're pushing sh*t uphill with a rubber toothpick!

If you want more guidance on creating the perfect Joint Venture for ANY business as a powerful FREE way to help your business grow, download my free JV Quick Start Guide where you'll discover:
- **How to find the right JV partners** - who to target and how to approach them.
- **A done-for-you outreach script** - exactly what to say to close the deal.
- **The irresistible JV offer formula** - make partners say *YES* instantly!

Download it FREE at www.nathanbaws.com/jvguide and start landing high-value JV deals today!

Dopamine Biohacking For Explosive Business Growth

The Bawsome 9 Business Growth Strategies are only good when they are put into practice and used daily.

That's where dopamine kicks in - fueling unstoppable drive, resilience, and problem-solving to power daily lead generation, sales and business growth. Ignore it and business becomes an uphill battle.

Tony Robbins (the business guru who endorses this book) talks about "getting into state" to master emotions and boost productivity. The good news is we can enhance this by biochemically optimizing dopamine to stay sharp, relentless, and ready for massive action. High dopamine fuels confidence, bold decisions, and discipline - everything you need to scale business faster.

Bawsome Dopamine Hacks for Peak Performance:

Activate dopamine throughout your day to unlock another level of Bawsome business success! (Sorry for the Bawsome overdose - when business is this good, regular words just don't cut it!)

Do as many of the following daily as possible to reach optimal dopamine levels:

- Cold Showers & Ice Baths - Instant energy boost & mental resilience. One of the biggest dopamine stimulants available. It's why I was involved in setting a Guinness Book of Worlds Record for ice baths in 2024.

- Exercise (Especially Endurance Training) - Fuels long-term motivation and fast dopamine secretion.

- Sunlight Exposure - Sharpens focus & lifts mood via dopamine.

- Celebrating Small Wins - Each success fuels a small dopamine hit and further enhances momentum.

- High-Protein & Fat Ketogenic Diet - Wildly powerful for stabilizing mood & maximizing brainpower via triggering ketones and dopamine (check out more on how to eat to optimize energy and brainpower for business growth at https://nathanbaws.com/the-business-growth-diet).

    It's crazy to think that diet has an impact on your business performance - but it does! Through optimizing your diet, you enhance physical endurance - so you can work for longer, faster and more productively in your workday, as well as elevating mental clarity. All essential for business growth.

- Meditation, Gratitude & Uplifting Music – Keeps motivation high through dopamine release.
- Avoid Dopamine Killers - Sugar is the worst of all evils but add junk food and mindless social media to this list.

Here is a bonus that might just blow your mind. In my keynote speeches I like to explore the link between dopamine stimulation and activating the law of attraction in business.

It's a concept few recognize, yet it plays a powerful role in generating business success. Stay tuned for another book to come related to the technical biochemical process involved, but the basics are as follows:

Dopamine directly influences the activation of the law of attraction. The esoteric book and film "The Secret," highlights how focused intention shapes reality and delivers the goods.

Few people understand that we can predictably, logically and formulaically activate the law of attraction by intentionally stimulating dopamine via natural biochemical modulation. In other words, we can boost dopamine to trigger a "flow state" - that amazing zone you tap into when everything flows smoothly and one positive event after the next comes into your life. Incredible business opportunities and outcomes then follow.

By optimizing dopamine levels, you heighten focus, confidence, and emotional intensity - key factors in aligning thoughts, actions, and energy with your goals. This biochemical shift enhances clarity, decision-making, and momentum, making you more receptive to opportunities while naturally attracting the right people, resources, and business breakthroughs.

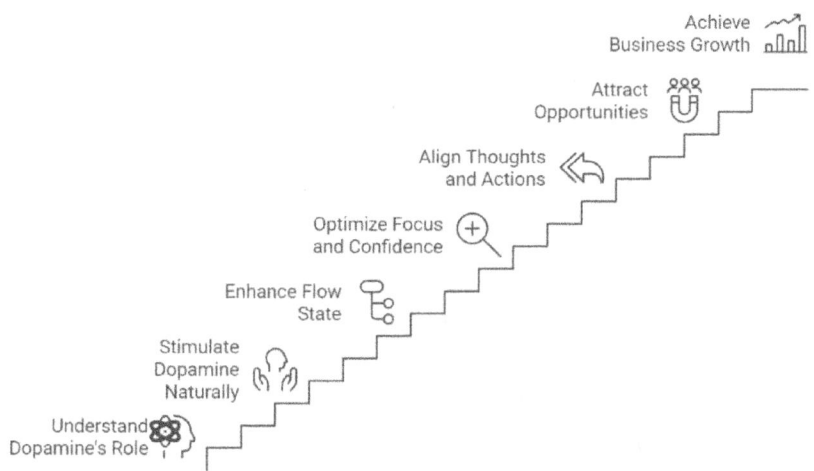

Dopamine is your businesses best friend. When strategically optimized, it can enhance customer acquisition, sales and unstoppable business growth.

Stack these habits, fire up your dopamine in a healthy manner and watch your business flourish!

If you want to grow your business and need some help, connect with me. Success favors those who take action, think bigger, and refuse to settle for potatoes!

**

Nathan Baws ND

Passionate Business Builder / Speaker / Author

Follow & Connect:

For high-impact strategies, powerful collaborations, and next-level business insights, visit www.nathanbaws.com and subscribe on YouTube to grow your business skills.

Facebook | @nathan.baws

Instagram | @nathanbaws

YouTube | @Nathan-Baws

www.nathanbaws.com

www.tommysugo.com.au

www.emersionwellness.com

www.businessprofitlab.com.au

www.flareschool.com

Available for keynote and virtual events on business growth, mindset optimization and dopamine-based performance strategies.

Rachel Baws

Rachel Baws, creative finance expert & speaker, is an investment bank escapee turned real estate investor with over 20 years of experience acquiring properties across four continents. Initially focused on single-family homes, she now concentrates on other asset classes - though her passion remains affordable housing. Always ahead of market trends, she has mastered nearly every strategy, including BRRRR, STR, MTR, LTR, Lease Options, Delayed Completions, Subject To, and Fix-And-Flips - often managing projects remotely. She thrives on structuring unconventional deals, creating value where others see limitations.

Having grown up with little, her love of creative finance was born out of necessity. She played a pivotal role in bringing innovative contract structures to the UK residential market, helping shape the legal framework many investors use today. With a large portfolio - mostly built through non-traditional financing - she has a knack for deal-making that prioritizes strategy over capital; strategies that are just as relevant to buying businesses as they are real estate.

Beyond investing, she's a sought-after keynote speaker, trainer, and author, blending real estate expertise with sharp insights into negotiation, human psychology, and risk-taking. She shares hard-won lessons on deal-making and decision-making, whether in high-stakes negotiations or haggling with her young niece and nephew—whom she considers the true master negotiators.

Based primarily in California, when she's not closing deals she's traveling, biohacking, learning, doing hot yoga and cold plunges.

From Candy Negotiations to Real Estate Millions

By Rachel Baws

Every day is a school day, no matter your age. And if you're an entrepreneur, an investor, or simply someone wanting to squeeze the most juice out of life, the lessons keep coming. They're everywhere. If you're missing them, you're either looking in the wrong direction… or hiding under a rock.

Forgive the bluntness. I'm an Aussie.

Pushing boundaries, getting out of comfort zones and taking calculated risks are my jam. I acquired $750,000 worth of real estate in under two years, without spending a dime of my own money. (That was just for starters). Stood on a stage and sung to an audience of over a thousand people. Skydived from 10,000 feet. Talked my way into prestigious investment banks, securing roles I was never 'qualified' for. (Not once.)

I've zip lined across gorges. Spoke on a real estate panel with more than 2000 people in attendance. Run marathons. Moved across the planet with no job, nowhere to live and just a few dollars in my pocket. Swam two miles through an African lake, unsure of what lay beneath. Negotiated with a three-year-old in a toy store, prying stuffed animals from her grip - knowing full well she'd unleash a nuclear meltdown if she didn't leave with them all. Bought properties sight unseen, and a decade later, still haven't set foot in some of them.

I haven't owned a TV for years. I don't watch the news. And that's no accident.

So why does this matter to YOU?

Because how you do anything… is how you do everything.

Or, put another way… *if you don't risk anything, you risk everything.*

Success in business – or the business of life - is not about recklessness; there's a degree of calculation involved. But here's the thing: you must be willing to pull the trigger even if you don't have all the answers. Jump in, adapt fast and figure it out along the way. You can't steer a parked car.

Not many of us have a crystal ball to rely on.

Have I stumbled along the way? Absolutely! Plenty of those stories for another day.

Most people wait. For the perfect moment. The perfect plan. The perfect guarantee. But here's the raw, undeniable truth:

If you want what everyone else has, do what everyone else does.

But if you want different, BE different.

Point made. Sermon over. For now.

Small town beginnings to Bigger Dreams

Born in remote, dusty northern Western Australia, my childhood was simple - riding bikes, playing outside until dark, usually running barefoot.

Then everything changed.

After my parents' divorce, my fiercely determined mother fought to keep a small, heavily mortgaged duplex. She rented out one side, we lived in the other. Interest rates were brutal. Money was tight.

Toys were few, but the adventures were endless.

We always had clothes on our backs (often homemade) and food on the table - though our diet consisted largely of rice and potatoes, and whatever we could get from the 'poor shop', a small store stocked with expired supermarket donations. We meditated daily and grew up listening to Tony Robbins and Zig Ziglar. We ate avocado before Instagram even knew it existed. Junk food? Limited. TV? Almost non-existent.

My first business – A captive market

Whenever my brother and I got our hands on a few coins, we sprint to the local store and agonize over which candy to buy. He'd devour his share before we even got home.

Then? He'd eye up mine.

Negotiations began - what was my stash worth to him?

I quickly learned about supply and demand, buying low and selling high. At just seven or eight years old, my first business was born. I had only one customer. A captive market is never a bad thing.

Thankfully any guilt about profiting off my brother has long since faded. I like to think we both gained valuable business lessons from those early negotiations. And considering Nathan has gone on to run multiple successful businesses – as he shares in his own chapter of this book – I'd say it all worked out. You're welcome, brother.

(I did apply a similar business model more widely in the school grounds several years later, with various other commodities.)

If a system works, why reinvent the wheel?

Eleven schools by age twelve – Adaptability is key

Perhaps it's not surprising I ended up in real estate - I spent more time moving than the average military family. Eleven schools by the time I was twelve. The constant upheaval made adaptability second nature, but we finally settled into our own home. It was the worst house on the best street we could afford. It even had a pool, although that was soon ripped out to plant a veggie patch. Much of the house was gutted too, but money dictated the renovation pace, so we lived on a construction site for years.

Despite financial struggles, education and reading were a priority. Many sacrifices were made to get us into good schools, where I was exposed to a world of wealth - mixing with politicians' and entrepreneurs' daughters. I saw sprawling mansions with internal waterfalls and lifts, and lifestyles that felt like something out of a dream.

It planted a seed.

By that time, I was devouring every adult book I could find - no, not *those* ones, thank you very much. Business, psychology, body language, wealth - mixed in with a bit of Wilbur Smith for balance. Not exactly your average pre-teen reading list, in hindsight.

The Wealthy had one thing in common – real estate.

With no handouts coming my way, I realized fast: if I wanted more, I had to create it myself. So I got my first official job at thirteen, working the cash register at a small store every Saturday. I held the job for five years and it funded my first flight to London - a trip that cemented my love for travel.

Lacking financial role models, I devised my own system - dividing my earnings into three envelopes: spend, save, and charity. Watching my savings balance grow gave me a thrill. I enjoyed school and loved languages. I threw myself into acting, dance, swimming, tennis, cross-country and more. I joined the mock trial team, playing at being a lawyer. University seemed like the logical next step, but home life was difficult, so I moved out at sixteen. I was accepted into university by the skin of my teeth.

But when I failed every subject, I did the only logical thing - packed my bags and moved to London with two suitcases and $800.

Bluffing my way into a career

Armed with a basic knowledge of admin work, self-taught touch typing, a bit of lipstick and a whole lot of nerve, I talked my way into a job at a prestigious property development firm. When people saw my fingers flying across the keyboard, they assumed I was experienced. I wasn't. But I became experienced. Fast.

I quickly mastered my role, took on extra work, and soon craved new challenges. I updated my resume and went after high-end placements - London's top law firms and investment banks - anywhere that paid well and moved fast. The short-term assignments became addictive, each role bringing new systems to learn and opportunities to grow and add value.

A three-week placement at Swiss Bank UBS was to work in a division setting up offshore trusts and structures for ultra-high-net-worth individuals. I was asked if I knew what that all meant (I didn't), but confirmed I did anyway, knowing I was resourceful and could figure it out as I went. Saying yes, I figured, was just me telling the truth in advance. (not a strategy I'd recommend if someone asks if you know how to perform brain surgery - unless of course you do).

Know your limits.

They went on to hire me full-time, and within a year I had risen to the C-suite, working closely with the Chairman. I was responsible for recruiting across a team of 300 employees, leading a large staff and managing high-profile clients. I received my first client gift - a Celine scarf. To an uninitiated 22-year-old, a service provider receiving lavish gifts felt backwards. My perspective was shifting again.

The First Real Estate Deal – a Joint Venture

A year later, my brother and I bought a property together - our first joint venture. I had a strong job on paper but little disposable income; he had cash flow but no "bankability". I hadn't seen the property, but it was just about numbers for me. We combined forces and got it done. I knew my time at UBS was limited, so I locked in the mortgage before moving on. A toxic work environment had made my role increasingly challenging, but back then, enduring it was just part of the game. I brushed it off, until enough was enough.

More short-term positions at other top investment banks followed, and then Goldman Sachs called. The position was a good fit, until they pushed me to go full-time. I declined, they begged, I eventually caved. The hours were brutal, but I worked alongside incredibly intelligent people.

Then came property number two, again sight unseen. Then another. Both inner-city properties overlooked the stunning Swan River - but like most Australian real estate transactions, they were negatively geared. No cash flow meant I had to subsidize the mortgage payments.

When I left Goldman's, my role was replaced by five people. Credit Suisse had headhunted me. I made it clear to them: I'd do my job, but I wouldn't work excessive hours. They hired me anyway, and within the first month I was on a flight from London to New York to meet the rest of my team. My first business class flight. It spoiled me for life.

I'd been in London for several years by now but still hadn't bought there. The UK real estate industry was archaic. (It still is) Gazumping and gazundering were commonplace. The idea of paying for valuations and surveys, only to have the seller back out at any time with no repercussions, terrified me. So, I slapped myself over the face and realized people bought and sold properties all the time—I could, too. After a couple of costly failed transactions, I secured my first London property: a three-bedroom apartment in Bow, East London. Once grimy, the area was strategically placed between two financial districts. Appreciation was inevitable.

Just before signing the paperwork on this purchase, doubts crept in. What if the tenant stopped paying? What if it stopped cash flowing? If needed, I'd move out of where I was still renting, into the Bow apartment and rent out the other rooms. If things went *really* south, I'd get another job. Hard work never scared me.

Then came the next property, and the next.

Creative Finance – Scaling Without Money

So how did I buy these properties if the little disposable income I had, was being used to pay the mortgages on the Australian properties? I got creative –

- Used 0% credit cards for deposits
- Rolled balances from one card to another
- Always repaid before the term ended
- Refinanced when possible, pulling out capital

Lender negotiations and debt restructuring became my specialty - though not by design. Since I know anyone else tackling real estate in the same way I was, I figured it out on the fly. Thankfully, the lenders didn't realize I was improvising.

I had to do it that way, to survive. Soon it became a superpower.

While at Credit Suisse, I accumulated more properties – even venturing into buying real estate in Europe too. I refined my processes, and systemized renovations. I learned how to hire and speak to contractors, assess their work, source materials, and - when necessary - do things myself. Years of often being the only woman in a boardroom, had prepared me well.

My formula made properties light, modern, and desirable for young professionals - my target market. And then, when the time came to leave the corporate world, I bought the most expensive house I could afford for myself to live in, while I could still get a mortgage.

It was a total reno job - six-weeks soon turning into multiple months. The contractors went bankrupt; suddenly I was the project manager. Three of the four floors were just exposed joists, and when you stepped in through the front door you could see the underside of the roof insulation – because there was nothing in between. I had crashed at a friend's place but ended up having to move into the only finished room in the house. My bed was a mattress on the floor, my kitchen a microwave perched on a box. Everything - me included - was covered in fine builder's dust for weeks. Stress levels? Off the charts.

And then the Global Financial Crisis hit, necessitating an immediate pivot. Much needed cashflow was created by switching some of the properties into short-term rentals, doing the Airbnb model before it was even a thing. Together with my brother, who had moved to London to invest in real estate, we began adapting creative finance strategies (commonplace with commercial deals) to the residential market. It took six months to refine our patterns of speech, then we closed three deals in a weekend. We were off the starting blocks.

When you solve others' problems, your own success takes care of itself

Traditional investing assumes you need cash or a bank loan to acquire assets. But what if you could structure deals that required neither? What if, instead of competing for the same limited pool of conventional deals, you could create opportunities others overlook?

Leveraging existing debt, negotiating seller financing so that they become the bank, or structuring performance-based payments meant I was able to scale my portfolio without tying up my own capital. While others were stuck waiting on financing or saving for down payments, I was doing deals others thought were impossible. And all this, years before 'Sub To' went mainstream. If existing debt rates are favorable, why extinguish one loan only to replace it with another?

One of the biggest mistakes investors make is assuming sellers only care about price. In reality, many are motivated by other factors -

steady income, a quick exit, or keeping a stake in what they've built. Understanding their true needs allows you to craft deals that benefit both sides. Listening to the seller becomes your competitive edge.

Rapidly, opportunities arose where others only saw roadblocks. Helping sellers who couldn't sell, creating a win-win.

One of the more rewarding deals, was with a family stuck in a tough spot. Their small house was underwater, and they were desperate to sell to move closer to relatives. The problem? The debt on the property was so high that even if they miraculously got an offer, they'd still have to bring money to the closing table - money they didn't have.

When we met, I offered them a way out. Instead of them paying to sell, I structured a deal that put a few thousand dollars in their pocket to help with their move. They walked away with relief instead of stress, and I took over the property, putting a tenant in place. Even though the house was in negative equity at the time, it cash-flowed, and I held onto it for eight years.

When I finally sold, that "underwater" house delivered a five-figured payday. Not bad for a deal most would've passed on.

If you know someone who can't sell, download my How to Make Money In Real Estate (Without Any Heavy Lifting) at: www.rachelbaws.com/real-estate-cash

Over time, demand for these strategies grew. We spent months in lawyers' offices refining contracts, and soon investors were seeking us out for guidance. Speaking engagements and training opportunities followed.

But as regulations tightened in the UK, it became clear that real estate investors were being penalized at every turn. It was time to focus on a market with more flexibility. The USA called.

Leverage & Joint Ventures: The Fastest Path to Scaling Wealth

Success in real estate - or any business - isn't about doing everything alone. As someone who did things primarily solo for a very long time, I can attest to the fact that the biggest wins come from leverage.

Leverage is key:

- Capital – Use other people's money if necessary. This includes existing debt.
- Time – Partnerships allow you to scale faster.
- Skills – If you lack a strength, bring in someone who has it.
- Connections – Deals are made through relationships.
- Systems – Automate or delegate repetitive tasks.
- Market Cycles – Timing can add extra $$$'s to a deal.
- Negotiation – Terms are often more important than price.
- Tax strategies – Keep more of what you earn using wealth-building tax systems.

The right JV partner changes everything. They fill any gaps. Maybe you have the deal, but not the funding. Or the skillset, but not the connections. A great JV lets each person bring something to the table, multiplying results.

Early in my career, I realized the power of leveraging existing debt, seller financing, and strategic partnerships to acquire assets without massive upfront capital. While others were saving for years to buy a single property, I was structuring deals that allowed me to scale quickly. Today, those same strategies apply to real estate, businesses and more. My focus is on multifamily, mobile home parks, RV Parks, residential portfolios, industrial spaces and hotels. But really, I love the art of structuring the deal - so if the numbers stack, I'll consider just about anything.

With a massive wave of baby boomer-owned assets about to hit the market, opportunities will soon be everywhere. Many sellers don't have a succession plan. They'd rather structure a deal that keeps their legacy intact while securing a steady income, often with tax benefits. Some might be fine handing over a chunk of their hard-earned income to Uncle Sam - but for those who'd rather keep more of what they've built, there's always a creative way to structure a deal!

So you bring the car - I'll add gas to the tank and put someone in the driver's seat.

Joint ventures = profit + fun. And let's be real - if we're enjoying the process, we're probably making better deals (and becoming better humans in the process). Sounds like a win-win to me!

If I can build a portfolio, you can too. Better yet, we could even do it together.

I haven't come this far, just to come this far.

Have you?

***

Rachel Baws

- Have capital to invest?
- Need a quick call to discuss a potential partnership?
- Got a deal but not sure how to negotiate or structure it?
- Need a fresh perspective, motivation, or a relatable voice for your next event?

Available for keynote speeches and virtual events on anything mindset or Real Estate related, with specific emphasis on Creative Finance for Real Estate and Business

Follow & Connect:

Website: www.rachelbaws.com

Connect: www.rachelbaws.com/connect

Facebook: www.facebook.com/RachelBaws

Instagram: @aussierachel

LinkedIn: www.linkedin.com/in/rachelbaws

Download: www.rachelbaws.com/real-estate-cash

Steve Higginbotham

Steve Higginbotham is The Coffee Coach - An accomplished business consultant and strategic visionary, leveraging four decades of expertise in Human Capital Solutions. He is a highly regarded advisor specializing in coaching and talent acquisition for leading organizations, ranging from Fortune 100 companies to mid-sized enterprises and startups. Renowned for delivering exceptional outcomes, he adds value through his transparent, collaborative approach. His talent for cultivating impactful partnerships consistently generates transformative results.

Steve has dedicated his career to coaching individuals in enhancing communication, fostering cohesive teams, resulting in outstanding customer engagements, uplifted workplace cultures, highly engaged teams, and improved leadership. In addition, Steve conducts speaking engagements and trainings which are informative, practical, creative, and impactful throughout the world.

Steve is a dedicated husband and father of three remarkable children, U.S. Navy Veteran, poet, an avid skateboarder, motorcycle enthusiasts, and enjoys finishing 70.3 Ironman triathlons. He has dedicated many years to helping Vets navigate post service job transitions.

Steve is a collaborative business partner and inclusive leader, helping to create lasting customer experiences. Steve's purpose is to help people through their struggles, in their careers and in life. He is big enough to matter and small enough to care. Steve has a proven history of developing, coaching, and mentoring individuals to become exceptional people.

BeYouToFull

by Steve Higginbotham (The Coffee Coach)

Be yourself to the fullest

BeYouToFull

Follow your dreams and let your heart lead the way – Steve Higginbotham

In order to have a full life, there are three main components that I believe one must have:

Passion. Purpose. Intent.

With these three things, you will create a healthy mindset and be rich in all aspects of your life - all of which will provide you with a fulfilling life.

Passion - To live a full life passionately, we need growth - to progress. What better way to grow than to invest in yourself? This investment needs to come from a place of positivity. In life, we all have struggles, challenges, oversights (hindsight's 20/20), get passed up for promotions, fall down, and just maybe need a helping hand from time to time. It's all a matter of perspective.

When you go through life and try new things, you're going to make mistakes. Focus on the lesson learned rather than the mistake. Consider yourself only bruised and not broken.

Bruises happen, and it's a sign of not sitting on the sidelines watching but being an active participant. In life, everything is not perfect. Life is about progression, not perfection.

Life is a gift, and we should cherish it. Don't waste it, and don't live it for someone else. Not for one second or one ounce of negativity. Focus on your passion. If you don't know what it is, then you'll need to find it.

What better way to be rich than to do all things from your heart?

Answer these two questions, and you can have a very successful, fulfilling, and rich life.

1. What do you want to do with YOUR LIFE?

   _____

2. What does success feel like for you?

   _____

There are many essential things in life, but the single most important thing is to get up and get

going. It's important to take notice that it's not that simple; one must get up with a clear, focused, and positive mindset. One of my first leaders, Wayne Gretzky, "The Great One," taught me something remarkably important. Preparation. While I was attending the Results 2000 seminar, which included Tony Robbins & Brian Tracy, I heard him speak about getting to the hockey rink early, prior to the game, and practicing - playing an entire game on the ice and in his head while skating around the rink. Mr. Gretsky was preparing for the game he was about to play and thinking about his opponents – visualizing and preparing hours before. He did this with every game. Mr. Gretsky's discipline and focus made him great at this game and allowed him to achieve many NHL records. He logged so many additional hours in his career than the average hockey player that no one could keep up with him. Mr. Gretsky was committed. He had such great vision and skills; they were unparalleled.

These are some of the important factors to pay attention to that will help shape your life into the person you dare to be and the person you wish you were.

LIFE - Living Individually Free Everyday

What exactly does that mean? There's no better way than to be empowered by yourself, to do what you love, with passion, for a greater purpose, and with intent.

Now, believe it. You've got to trust in yourself. Identify who you are. That's that IT factor.

Individual Talents.

Using your Individual Talents and your passion to make an impact in this world. Now that's a life worth pursuing! You could consider the following avenues.

- Relationships
- Careers
- Self-Development
- Self-Care
- Serving others

Example: You could have a better, deeper, and more meaningful relationship with those you love, hence creating a more positive impact in this world. Even greater than you could image. The same goes for your career; if you come to work with positivity, you are more likely to radiate a positive vibe, which people can receive and embrace. The same goes for coming home from work; if you're positive and love your job, boss, and/or company, you are more likely to be positive when leaving work and return home, where your loved ones can also receive a greater sense of positivity from you.

Be the leader in your life, living positively with passion, and having a greater purpose to serve others in all aspects of your life (career, family, relationships, community, etc).

Servant Leadership is more than just serving others; it's a mindset. Approaching every task or situation with, "How can I serve?" It's about having this healthy mindset and infusing it into every aspect of your life. Serving moves you from the I mentality, yourself, to the we mentality, others.

Being a servant leader starts from your heart and ultimately helps you answer the character question: Who are you as a human being?

In business, the #1 customer to serve are the people around you, in a department, group, team, and the entire company. The #1 customer in life is your loved ones, your family, and community. By serving them, take care of your people, and your life will be much richer. Sometimes, it's as simple as a phone call away (or, in today's world, a text message away). Show them you care. Let them know you want them in your life. The best bosses that I've worked with and for all have approachability. Allowing someone to approach them with an open-door policy and truly meaning it, living by it, and encouraging it. These are the leaders who are truly servants. In addition, the best leaders let people know they care about them. It's as easy as walking up to the person and saying "thank you" for a task well done, writing them a note, or mailing them a postcard when you're traveling for business. It must come from the heart. Equally important is saying "thank you" in public, at a board meeting, or in an all-hands meeting - praising people publicly. You'll know when it's right to thank a person because it's rarely wrong.

Purpose - Having purpose in life is one of the richest things I have ever experienced. Purpose is that great feeling you get when your passion shapes your sense of meaning and direction in life, contributing to you having a fulfilling life.

It's OK to DREAM BIG ... even BIGGER. Just *STOP* fooling yourself into thinking your DREAMS are going to come true without working hard towards them, making sacrifices, shifting your mindset, elevating your career, and adjusting your habits.

A purposeful life will help you wake up and focus on the things that matter most to you. Start working towards that big dream. No one's going to do it for you!

Purpose is also being rich in everything you do - putting your passion, not anyone else's, your passion into it. You don't have to have a greater purpose, but it sure does help. And doing it intentionally is equally important.

In life, I've come to realize that everything starts from and leads back to the heart. *It's the center of intention.*

Your mindset, relationships, your social circles, the amount of effort you put into your job or career, and the money you make doing all of this, well, it's all heart. Purpose comes from the heart. Having a greater purpose comes from and lives within the heart.

Look at your career choices and see if you have held positions where you were living out a fulfilling job, handling responsibilities that were meaningful to you and impacted those around you in a positive manner. Was this a job or a career? Did you do this with passion and purpose? Or was this centered around money, holding a certain title, or were you doing it just because you wanted that promotion?

Having an illustrious career requires many things, which we will not go into now. However, the feeling from that distinguished career or position we will address. Consider one of your great positions, a job, or maybe even your current career. What is the feeling you receive, not just for a job well done, but rather knowing that you are contributing to the greater good of a team, department, and company? Knowing this feeling can all be different during the course of your career, yet the common factor in your life is a feeling from the heart, and does it leave you fulfilled?

Career transition can be very scary. However, if you are a life-long learner like me, you should embrace it. Yes, it can be disruptive, although each time you transition, there's always a lesson to be learned in the process, sometimes many lessons. You could be learning a new skill, gaining valuable project knowledge, and keeping this within your arsenal for the next career opportunity or promotion. If you ever find yourself without a meaningful job, working within a company that doesn't appreciate you, you know who to reach out to. Never work for an unappreciated leader and certainly not a poor boss. There's always a better job out there. Don't be fooled into thinking this is your only security due to the market conditions. I've seen some pretty devastating market conditions and I've been able to help people find jobs, myself included. Navigating a career transition is a significant LIFE-changing (altering) event, not only for you, your significant other/partner, and even your family, as well as your company. Believe it or not, turnover impacts the company more than you could imagine. It can be scary; however, if this is your intent and you are well-prepared, it can be rewarding and fulfilling. More people suffer from stress at work than in any other area in life, except for money. If you have a well-planned career path and you find purpose and meaning in your job, most likely you'll not be one of those people, as money will come based on your level of success at work, a by-product of you loving your work, and being passionately engaged. Money comes to those who are invested in their career, making a positive impact and contributing greatly (having a great purpose) to the overall success of the company.

All of this makes for a healthy and happier you, contributing to your life and helping you to progress and feed your passion. This all works together and stems from your mindset, passion in your work and life, value and purpose, and intent. Although stress can come from many areas, money is one of the major contributing factors. And your career, or well-being at work, makes a huge difference. If you had a rewarding and impactful job/career, you would most likely be way more fulfilled in life, contributing to your bottom line and the money you make from the magnificent work you provide. From the past three and a half decades that I have served this world, working in many jobs, supporting many companies, observing, watching, listening, and coaching hundreds of people, I have found that staying at a job you dislike, one that does not support your passion or purpose is not healthy or fulfilling.

Gallup (in a recent poll) states that 85% of people are unhappy in their jobs, and only 15% state that they are engaged. If I'm a leader, this is devastating to the growth of the company. If I'm an individual, this is appalling.

The three main reasons people remain at the jobs in which they dislike are as follows:

- Fear of change
- Lack of better opportunities
- Financial security

FEAR is the major culprit.

It's important to work in your business as much as it is to work on it. The difference is that working in your business is taking action and doing tasks even if they are not producing results; today, you still need to be consistent and persistent even if you don't want to. One of the best phrases that I have ever heard comes from the US Navy SEALs – *You don't got to love it, you just got to do it.* Working on your business is thinking, reflecting, strategizing, trying to grab hold of that edge, getting ahead and with the intent to focus on who you are going to become and what you would like to accomplish the next task and how you are shaping yourself to help put your business in the right position to be successful.

The solution for all of us, myself included, is to act, do something. Start working and stop wishing for success. Wake up and work hard towards your dreams. Start living your life with intent. The easiest way to live intentionally is to communicate well while serving others.

Communication is the backbone of any relationship. You have heard the saying – it's not what you know. It's who you know. *Level Up* your network, and you will go places you've never been. Have a career you never thought was possible. Make more money. Do all of this with passion, purpose, and intent; you'll have a rich, fulfilling life.

Relationships are intentional. Everyone wants something out of them, even if they're serving others. The one serving gets more from the reward of feeling good afterwards, which is the intent. Give your time, money, and skills and direct them towards helping people. They all start with care, infused with love, and are transformed by how much care and love you pour into them or not. Relationships are a two-way street; they work both ways, just like a phone call or text message. To have a relationship, there must be an exchange, a give, a take, and the transfer of caring back and forth, not just one way. If you find yourself in a one-way relationship, meaning you are giving and not receiving, you might just want to ask yourself - is this a meaningful relationship, and is it what I want and/or need for myself? Self-care means walking away from bad situations, people, and jobs. Having a RICH relationship always requires your heart to be involved. Relationships worth having are worth putting 100% care and effort into, with passion, purpose, and intent; otherwise, it's not a relationship; it's a [fill in the blank], whatever you want to call it.

Your relationships, the people you most associate yourself with, hold the keys to your success. Knowledge speaks; *wisdom* listens. In relationships, it's also important to be an active listener. Just being there for someone can be fulfilling. Remember to serve others. Just make sure you are being served, as well.

If you approach life by simply asking intelligent questions and listening to those around you, you can find out the majority of what you need to know on your own through self-awareness. However, if you *Level Up*, your circle and ask intelligent questions to your relationships, you'll get so much more out of these conversations by being more passionately engaged. Knowing there is so much more, rich discussions and deeper conversations to be had. All the answers you ever need are within your realm. The universe has a unique way of displaying them. You must recognize the opportunities and take full advantage of them.

Level Up your circle - Be surrounded by people in all aspects of your life who help you elevate your talents. Increase your community and rise above mediocrity to move from the cloudiness of theory and the stress of wondering into the clarity of doing.

Intent - If you are not truly feeling happy in any aspect of the above, you can simply course correct or change your direction entirely to make a greater impact in your life. It's very simple, but this might not be easy.

Speak encouraging thoughts to yourself. Do not ponder over what went wrong; instead, focus on what you learned and gained from each experience. I've learned hundreds and hundreds of lessons throughout my career and life, yet something as simple as a Friday Night T-Ball game, 1-hour, I learned something new (ask me about it). If you're open to learning, there are lessons to be learned in the simplest of tasks. There are hundreds of lessons to learn right in front of you if you have the self-awareness and an open heart to see and receive them.

Take Action !! Be intentional about improving yourself.

Focus on you!

Serve your circles ~ The fact that no one is unscathed by their work is kind of a blessing. What do I mean by this? Wherever you are today and in whatever direction you go, there is a need that has never been as profound as it is right now. The best news of all is that you are there in a way that no one else is and certainly in a way that I'm not.

So, here's the deal: Get up every day with determination and decide who you want to be. Focus only on today. Do this with the intent of living a fulfilling, rich life with passion and purpose.

Now more than ever, you have the means. Everything is only a few keystrokes away - everything is within your proximity!

Today, you have the time, talents, means, and resources necessary to fulfill whatever you want. All you need to do is take the first step and embrace these core principles that have inspired extraordinary action.

Become a warrior, not a worrier.

Every moment of every day, you have a choice - you get to decide - who you are right now.

Make a declaration to yourself and determine who you are going to be.

Dare to be who you wish you were.

Believe in **you**rself. *BE YOU* to the fullest – *BeYouToFull*.

***

To contact Steve:

Email: thecoffeecoach@stevehiggy.com

Website: www.stevehiggy.com

LinkedIn: https://www.linkedin.com/in/stevehiggy/

YouTube: https://www.youtube.com/@SteveHiggyTheCoffeeCoach

Reginald G. Jackson, Sr.

Reginald G. Jackson, Sr. is the Principal Coach and Founder of Total Brilliance Coaching, a coaching and consulting firm located in the Washington, D.C. metro area. He offers clients more than four decades of leadership development and training experience, serving twenty years as an active-duty Marine. As a Professional Certified Coach (PCC) credentialed by the International Coaching Federation, his clients include emerging leaders, senior executives, and uniformed service members transitioning to veteran status. Along with supporting individuals through various stages of personal and professional growth, he also works alongside leadership teams as they navigate the challenges of strategic planning and organizational change management. With an extensive background in IT Project Management, his knowledge of risk management, operations, and process improvement makes him a valuable resource. Able to navigate fast-paced environments and climates of constant change, Reginald helps his clients turn chaos into clarity through systems and processes.

Align Your Focus with Your Intention

By Reginald G. Jackson, Sr.

In today's world of demands, disturbances, and distractions, it's no surprise we sometimes find ourselves peppered with anxiety. There just doesn't seem to be enough hours in the day. The problem is there is more demand than there is time. Raise your hand if you've ever been in a meeting (virtual or in person) and start reading a message on your phone or perhaps diverting your attention to email. You can think of a thousand other things that are far more important. You don't even know why you're in the meeting in the first place. There you are - bored out of your mind. It's like watching paint dry or grass grow. And so, you drift off into your own world. Out of nowhere, your name is called, and you're snatched back into the meeting.

Startled and embarrassed, with full attention now drawn to your more than obvious absence, you asked to have the question repeated. Maybe you even admitted you weren't listening. Busted! Congratulations on being the subject of multitasking at its best. Practically everyone is familiar with the "art" of multitasking. Some may even boast about their ability to do several things at once. Although it's possible to do more than one thing at a time, like walking while talking, the amount of cognitive effort necessary to do something well requires far more focus than one would think. Unfortunately, not only is multitasking a myth, but the illusion of its possibility is the furthest thing from the truth. What **is** true is that it causes us to perform well below the level of excellence we're capable of when we devote our focus to a single function. Multitasking winds up being a colossal waste of time and energy.

Leaders are desperate to find ways to manage their workload, lead their teams, and accomplish the mission. Not to mention the added responsibility of making sure their team is fully equipped to achieve success. Needless to say, the struggle is real. There must be a solution, right? Enter productivity hacks. There's no mistaking the fact that countless experts offer programs and/or solutions, books, videos, and workshops highlighting the importance of productivity and the perfect tool to get you there. If you could only find the right solution, it would solve your problems. While I don't discount or discredit what's out there, choosing what works for you can be overwhelming. There is an alternative for those who have found themselves completely dissatisfied after purchasing solutions that didn't work. It's less about the solution and more about the approach. That's why sometimes we could all use a little help.

As an executive coach, it's not unusual for my clients to share their frustration regarding having too much to do and insufficient time to finish it. The essence of my coaching philosophy is to help my clients turn chaos into clarity through systems and processes. This is a simple concept that can even be considered a framework. It has become a mantra of sorts: **Align your focus with your intention**. Six simple words, easily remembered, that can be incredibly powerful. Before I share the details of this framework, it's worth offering a bit of context to understand how it came to be.

A few years ago, I had a session with a long-time client. We worked together for several years and established a great rapport. With each promotion or increase in responsibility, her organization provided coaching to support the development of her leadership and management skills. I had witnessed her rise in the organization, excelling every step of the way. She had an uncanny gift for identifying and analyzing trends. It was like being the proverbial canary in the coal mine. Whenever she would sound the alarm, alerting senior leadership of her prediction, the challenge was appropriately articulating it in a way that resonated. During the call, she shared her struggle with how to craft the presentation in a way that would deliver a compelling message that could get the point across without being too technical or "in the weeds." With a look of exasperation, she said, "I have writer's block and don't know how to move past it. I can't ever remember feeling this stuck before." I encouraged her to distill her thoughts and identify the core message she wanted to get across. I also asked what it was she wanted them to know, emphasizing the importance of being intentional. In the silence that followed, I simply said, "You need to align your focus with your intention." What came next was something I will always remember. "Wait! Say what you just said again!" After repeating it, I watched the light bulb come on. Then she uttered these words. "That's so simple, yet it's so powerful. It makes so much sense! If only I had known this 30 years ago it would have made things so much easier." We both had a good laugh. As the laughter subsided, I realized a shift was occurring. The grin slowly faded, and her gaze became fixed on an object only she could see. Then, the typing began. It wasn't unusual for her to take notes on her computer. However, this time, it was more than just notes.

I sat quietly, honoring the silence, allowing her to capture her thoughts. During the silence, I had my own period of reflection. Coaching is much more than asking questions and making observations. It's also being a thought partner, co-creating a space that invites awareness, exploration, and discovery. Being a witness to that is indescribable. While it wasn't the first time I had seen a client experience a breakthrough or gain greater clarity, it was the first time I had seen words come to life in that way. I could actually "see" the focus AND the intention. A minute or so later, she returned from her musing and quietly said, "Okay. I think I have enough to go on. I'll finish this later." That session marked the birth of a mantra I continue to share to this day.

Now that context has been established, what does 'Align your focus with your intention' mean, and how can you apply it? First, we need to define each element.

Align(ment)

Being aligned (or in alignment) is like an agreement. It's a connection between two things, just like a bridge, which is a structure that allows passage from one side to the other. The connection also represents congruence. In this case, there is a consistency of thought related to the behavior, the action, and the outcome. All things are working together toward a common goal.

Focus

Focus is the act of concentrating or paying particular attention to a thing or a concept. It is the center of your thoughts, a singular interest, which can sometimes be so strong you can lose sight of everything else around you. Your ability to think and stay connected to that thought is the key. Focus can also include others, such as collaborating on a project or engaging in a conversation to produce an outcome or resolve an issue. While it doesn't require hours of isolation or solitude, success will likely follow when you establish and maintain an uninterrupted or undisturbed train of thought or activity.

Intention

Your intention is the purpose, plan, or objective you have in mind. Depending on the situation, it can even equate to a value or an equally important ideology. You should also take into consideration the nature of your intention. To determine this, there are a few questions to consider. What is the motivation? In other words, what makes the intention important in the first place? Another question to ask is, what is your relationship to your intention? Are you committed to the intention, or is it something you could do without? What benefit is the outcome? Does it make a difference? If so, it's most likely a worthy candidate. For example, an intention could be positioning yourself for the next stage of your career. Or maybe it's a health goal. Simply put, the intention has meaning and value.

The Situation

Imagine a boat without an engine or a rudder. It lacks the ability to steer or travel in a desired direction. Now, imagine you're a passenger on that boat. You'd be forced to travel wherever the current takes you, having no control of where you end up. In still waters, you would simply float, perhaps going nowhere. While this is merely an analogy, I would venture to say at one time or another, you may have felt this way before: wandering aimlessly with an undetermined destination. Think back to a time when you felt stuck or were frustrated because you had no real goal in mind. You were desperately searching for purpose, joy, or fulfillment. What was most evident is that you found it difficult to get past that feeling of being stuck or frustrated. Toward the end of the day or during the weekend, you weren't doing much more than drifting into a repeated pattern that felt like treading water. Perhaps that time is now. In the absence of intention, it's not unusual to get caught up with aimless hobbies like a Netflix binge or scrolling through social media. When it comes to social media, you also want to be mindful about what you're consuming. Sometimes, exercising a little escapism has its benefits. While I'm not suggesting anything wrong with setting aside time to decompress, it neither accomplishes a goal nor produces an outcome that moves you forward. If you find you're doing this on a regular basis, it's worthwhile investigating that pattern. Having a plan (or a framework) can make all the difference. For instance, aligning your focus with your intention.

The Solution (example)

Isiah has been given the opportunity of a lifetime. He pitched his company to a group of investors interested in his product. He understands his market and has been successful in scaling his business to a level he once thought was unattainable. The task at hand is to create a presentation that clearly and succinctly articulates his vision (intention). The presentation is to be delivered in two weeks' time. This is something he's been working toward for quite a while, and now it's up to him to deliver. Knowing full well he needs to devote the next few days to refining his presentation, he finds himself distracted and filled with doubt. What if they don't like his presentation? What if they don't think it's worthy of their investment? What if he's been fooling himself all along? They will most likely refuse the idea once they see it for what it really is. As each day passes, he finds it more difficult to stay on task. He's worried. As a matter of fact, he's more frightened than he's been in recent memory. Finally, in a moment of frustration, he says out loud, "What am I doing? I need to align my focus with my intention." He suddenly realizes how far away he is from the task at hand. Although he's fully aware he should be putting the final touches on the presentation (intention), he has allowed himself to spiral into self-doubt and despair (focus). He also concludes that he needs to quiet the noise and concentrate (focus) on including all the elements he knows are necessary to make the presentation successful (intention). For the next few days, Isaiah is dedicated to creating a presentation that clearly and succinctly identifies all the salient points he knows will convince the investors that his company is worthy of their investment, and it will yield the anticipated return. He has placed all his efforts into creating the end result. While the outcome has yet to be determined, this demonstrates aligning focus with intention.

When we consider Isaiah's thoughts and beliefs, it's clear he initially doubted himself. He questioned the value and worth, not only of his company but also of himself. While he was aware of his intention, he focused on self-doubt and failure. There was no alignment between his focus (self-doubt and failure) and delivering a powerful and compelling presentation to secure investment capital (intention). By pausing to notice his disruptive train of thought, he was able to remind himself about the mantra. He then shifted his negative mindset, realizing it was inconsistent with the task at hand, which was designing the presentation.

The key to success is to notice when you're out of alignment. Needless to say, it requires practice and discipline. With regularity and consistency, you'll discover a more frequent interruption of disparate thoughts and unproductive internal discourse. Whenever you find yourself feeling stuck, frustrated, or disorganized, you can always rely on those six compelling words to help you find your equilibrium. Just remember to align your focus with your intention.

This is but one of many examples of how I help organizational leaders, and their teams effectively address the demands of their environment and conquer uncertainty. By identifying themes and patterns, I teach them to implement tools and resources that are practically situation-agnostic. Together, we turn chaos into clarity through systems and processes.

***

To contact Reggie:

To learn more about Total Brilliance Coaching:

Visit my website

https://www.totalbrilliancecoaching.com

Connect with me on LinkedIn

https://www.linkedin.com/in/coachreginaldgjacksonsrpcc/

Listen to my podcast - It's Hard Because We Say It Is™ with Coach Reggie

https://open.spotify.com/show/4Hsr11vfPgHOgT4lexLNOh

Stevi Gable Carr

Stevi Gable Carr is the Founder + CEO of WISe Wellness Guild, a consultancy + media agency aimed at advancing humans through whole-self wellness. WISe Wellness Guild serves as a trusted partner to corporations such as Kroger, P&G, FIS, Fifth Third Bank, TH Foods, KAO, and many more, offering strategic growth consultation, consumer & market insights, programming, advertising, and access to a community of over 60,000+ wellness consumers in 50 US states and nine countries. Notably, WISe also serves over 600 women and minority-owned wellness businesses, driving intersectionality in wellness by connecting them to both corporations and consumers.

Carr has over 20 years of brand-building experience at companies like P&G, Newell Rubbermaid, and UC Health. As a working mother and engaged community member, Carr is a fierce advocate for supporting the retention in the workforce. Carr is a Board Member of the P&G Alumni Network, Fellow- Institute of Coaching, McLean/ Harvard Medical School, is an on-air expert for iHeart Radio, and serves as Ambassador to Global Wellness Institute. Recently, Stevi Gable-Carr was featured in Forbes, Entrepreneur, and Fortune Magazines, named P&G Alumni Association Visionaries Under 40 Honoree, a 2020 Cincinnati Business Courier's 40 Under 40 Honoree, 2020 Women Who Mean Business Honoree and Venue's 2022 Influential Women of Cincinnati

Audacious By Design:
6 Audacious Acts to Fuel Legacy Through Well-being

By Stevi Gable Carr

Let's get real—most leaders chase legacy the way they chase success: grinding, achieving, and building something they hope will outlast them. But here's the real question: Is the legacy you're building aligned with the life you want to live?

Society has drilled it into us—leadership demands sacrifice, and success requires burnout. But what if that's the biggest lie we've been sold? What if well-being isn't a luxury—it's the foundation of sustainable leadership? Energy, focus, and resilience aren't just personal perks; they're non-negotiables for leaders who want to make a lasting impact. You can't inspire, innovate, or influence if you're running on fumes. When you're depleted, so is your business. So is your team. So is your ability to create real change.

Your legacy isn't about following someone else's roadmap—it's about having the courage to rewrite it. The most radical act of leadership is ensuring that your success isn't just about external accomplishments but about building a life and legacy that actually align with your values. It's refusing to let outdated expectations dictate how you lead.

The leaders who leave the deepest legacies aren't the ones who push the hardest—they're the ones who lead with clarity, vitality, and purpose. And they don't get there by accident. They had the audacity to design their lives and to make choices that challenged everything we've been taught about success.

In this chapter, you'll learn the Six Audacious Acts to relentlessly pursue an impactful and sustainable legacy. It's not about pushing harder—it's about leading smarter. This is about power moves that make success and well-being non-negotiable. It's not about balance—it's about leverage. Because the most audacious act you can take isn't grinding until you break—it's having the courage to build a legacy that won't break you.

Redefining Success

Success isn't just about external accomplishments—it begins with internal alignment and, ultimately, fulfillment. Many leaders set business milestones, believing these achievements will eventually lead to their envisioned life. But what if you flipped the script? Decide what truly matters to you today instead of working toward some future version of happiness. What priorities will maximize the impact of your time on Earth? How can you align your personal and professional life to support them?

Discovering Your Values

Your values are your compass—they guide how you show up, make decisions, and sustain yourself through challenges. According to Intentional Change Theory (ICT), developed by Dr. Richard Boyatzis, sustainable personal and professional growth is achieved through deliberate self-awareness, goal-setting, and aligned action. To become a sustainable leader, you must have the audacity to design your life with intention, ensuring that your values are not just abstract concepts but actionable drivers of change.

"Knowing yourself is the beginning of all wisdom"- Aristotle.

The approach I most often use with executive coaching clients is intentional change theory. I believe that meaningful transformation begins by identifying your "ideal self"—the version of you that aligns with your core values and aspirations. This clarity has empowered clients to

- Navigate challenges
- Stay focused
- Develop an authentic, sustainable leadership style.

By intentionally aligning their lives and careers with their personal values, they have built and led multi-billion-dollar businesses while creating a lasting legacy.

Why wouldn't you invest the same level of care and strategy in your personal life that you pour into your business? Prioritizing well-being and values alignment isn't just about being a better leader—it's about building a more meaningful and enduring legacy.

Audacious Act #1: Name What Matters

Define your top 3-5 core values. Identify what truly lights you up. Pinpoint what brings you joy in the moment and look to your past for clues. Align your actions with your values, and identify where your current behaviors don't match your ideal self. Close the gap. Live with intention.

Sustainable Leadership is Rooted in Whole-Self Wellness

Like many leaders, I once equated success with relentless hustle—at the expense of my well-being. I learned the hard way that sustainable success isn't possible without prioritizing well-being and energy. I pushed through exhaustion, took work calls from a hospital bed after emergency surgery, and sent an email minutes after witnessing gun violence. I thought I was leading with resilience—I was really just surviving.

Chasing a promotion at my so-called "dream job," I hit a breaking point. Burnout forced me to step away, but that space gave me clarity. I redefined leadership on my terms, prioritized my whole-self wellness, and realized that if I wanted to build a legacy of impact, I had to lead differently. I couldn't follow the leadership models I had once admired—I had to create a new one.

From that reckoning, I built the WISe Wellness Guild and multiple seven-figure businesses—not by grinding harder but by leading smarter. I stopped choosing between success and well-being and embraced "yes–and." I can manage global clients and speak to thousands while also being a kindergarten room mom and hosting friends for a hike. True impact isn't about outworking everyone—it's about leading with energy, clarity, and the discipline to protect what fuels you.

Well-being is a Verb

We have to create space for our wellness *before* we're forced to make time for our sickness. If we want to break barriers and forge new paths, we need the strength to punch through them.

Sustainable leadership is built on eight pillars of whole-self wellness, each reinforcing the other to fuel resilience, clarity, and impact. Physical wellness powers performance through movement, nutrition, and rest, while emotional wellness strengthens self-awareness and resilience. Intellectual wellness drives continuous growth, and social wellness reminds us that success is never a solo journey. Spiritual wellness keeps leaders anchored in purpose, while occupational wellness aligns work with passion for lasting fulfillment. Environmental wellness shapes focus and energy through intentional surroundings, and financial wellness provides the stability to lead with confidence. Neglect one, and the foundation weakens—prioritize them all, and you build a lasting legacy.

Leaders face constant pressure to juggle professional demands while maintaining personal well-being. Every pillar of health—whether physical, emotional, or financial—interconnects, forming the foundation of *sustainable* success. Prioritizing one area while neglecting the rest doesn't work. True balance comes from small, consistent habits that build long-term resilience.

The Power of Small Actions

Success isn't built in a single moment. It's the result of stacking small, consistent actions over time. Legacy is no different. As James Clear puts it, *"Every action you take is a vote for the type of person you wish to become."*

The best leaders don't *hope* for change—they *create* it by designing habits that align with their values and long-term goals.

Step 1: Reflect – Identify which habits support or hinder your growth.

Step 2: Take Action – Stack habits, set micro-goals, and embrace feedback as fuel.

Step 3: Sustain Momentum – Track progress, celebrate small wins, and adjust when needed.

Because leadership—and life—isn't about intensity. It's about *consistency.*

Audacious Act #2: Seek Radical Feedback

Want to fast-track your growth? Reach out to someone you admire—a leader, mentor, or peer—and ask for honest feedback on one area where you can focus on improvement.

Yes, it might feel uncomfortable. But real growth starts when you stop playing small and actively seek the insights that will push you forward.

The leaders who make the biggest impact aren't the ones who never fail.

They're the ones who refuse to quit.

Energy Management and Burnout Prevention

Burnout isn't a badge of honor—it's a leadership liability that weakens decision-making, kills creativity, and drains presence. The truth? You don't just need more time—you need more energy and intentionality around how you spend your energy. Ignoring burnout doesn't just drain your energy; it weakens decision-making, kills creativity, and diminishes leadership presence.

According to Gallup, employees with poor well-being face a 61% higher risk of burnout—and leaders are no exception. If you want to build something sustainable and impactful, you need to own your energy before burnout steals your momentum.

Breaking the Burnout Cycle

Burnout doesn't happen overnight—it sneaks in through exhaustion, irritability, and decision fatigue. Get proactive with science-backed strategies that fuel resilience and performance:

- **Optimize Ultradian Rhythms**: Your brain cycles through 90- to 120-minute focus peaks. Instead of pushing through exhaustion, align deep work with peak energy and take short, intentional recovery breaks to reset cognitive function.

- **Leverage Creative Fatigue**: Innovation happens when you step away. Slight fatigue enhances unexpected connections (those "aha" moments in the shower). Shift gears—doodle, listen to music, free-write—and let your subconscious solve your problem.

- **Upgrade Your Rest**: Mindless scrolling doesn't recharge you. Instead, use high-impact recovery like NSDR (Non-Sleep Deep Rest), a neuroscience-backed technique that mimics sleep's repair processes for faster cognitive recovery or laughter & play; dopamine-driven, pressure-free activities reduce stress, fuel resilience, and enhance decision-making.

Make energy management a leadership strategy. Schedule energy audits for yourself and your team, embed micro-recovery into workflows and train your organization to work with human performance cycles, not against them.

Audacious Act #3: Reclaim Your Sense of Self

Defy the myth that constant connectivity equals productivity. Your greatest leadership asset is not your time—it's your energy.

- *Disconnect for 24 Hours. No emails. No social media. No work calls.*

- *Engage in restorative activities—movement, deep rest, laughter, play, or uninterrupted time with people who fuel you.*

- *Protect your energy like you protect your bottom line—because without it, both suffer.*

Your legacy depends on your ability to lead with clarity, intention, and presence.

The best leaders don't just manage time—they master energy.

Your Inner Circle Shapes Your Legacy

Leadership isn't just about what you build—it's about who you build it with. Every great leader understands that their environment influences their growth as much as their own actions. Yet, under relentless pressure from customers, investors, employees, and even family, many leaders neglect the energy and people they allow into their orbit.

Take a moment to assess: Who holds you accountable for your growth and well-being? Who challenges your thinking, pushes you forward, and ensures that your habits align with the legacy you're building?

The Price of Prioritization: Disappointing People

Here's a hard truth: If you're committed to your growth, you will disappoint people. No matter how clearly you communicate your vision, set boundaries, or bring value to those around you, someone will feel let down. And that's okay.

The Myth of Universal Approval

High achievers often fall into the trap of people-pleasing—chasing validation, avoiding conflict, and maintaining harmony. But the moment you start prioritizing your goals, your well-being, and your vision, you disrupt the status quo.

- When you stop overextending yourself, some people will get frustrated.
- When you redefine success on your terms, others will resist.
- When you say no to what no longer serves you, some will take it personally.

This isn't failure—it's leadership with integrity.

The Fear of Disappointment vs. The Cost of Self-Betrayal

Too many leaders hesitate to enforce boundaries, take bold action, or pivot in ways that serve their highest potential. But here's the real question:

What's the greater cost—disappointing others or betraying yourself?

Research backs this up. A study published in *Frontiers in Human Neuroscience* found that people often change their decisions to avoid the discomfort of disappointing others. Some cave at the first sign of pushback, while others with higher resilience stay the course and achieve better outcomes.

The takeaway? Disappointment is inevitable, but resilience determines success. The leaders who build lasting legacies aren't the ones avoiding friction. They're the ones who stand firm, take risks, and accept that outgrowing relationships, expectations, and outdated versions of themselves are part of the journey.

Redefining Disappointment: A Sign of Growth

If you disappoint people, it means you're growing, setting boundaries that protect your energy, aligning decisions with your purpose, and choosing depth over surface-level approval.

Not everyone will understand. Not everyone will celebrate your choices. But the ones who belong in your life—those who respect and support your vision—will adjust. And those who don't? They were never meant to be permanent fixtures in your path.

Audacious Act #4: Make Peace with Disappointing People

Where have you been holding back in your leadership or personal life out of fear of disappointing others? Write down one bold decision you know you need to make but have hesitated due to external expectations. Now, commit to taking action.

- *Set the boundary.*
- *Walk away from the draining commitment.*
- *Realign with your true priorities.*

True leadership isn't about making everyone happy. It's about making decisions that allow you to lead with authenticity, impact, and sustainable well-being.

The moment you embrace this, you stop seeking permission—and start building your legacy with confidence.

Your Network is Your Foundation: Why You Need an Executive Coach

"You are the average of the five people you spend the most time with." It's not just a cliché—it's a leadership principle.

Who you surround yourself with directly impacts your mindset, decisions, and legacy. If your environment is filled with stress, scarcity, and reactive decision-making, that energy seeps into your leadership. But when you intentionally curate a circle of growth-driven, purpose-focused individuals, you accelerate your success, resilience, and impact.

The most successful and fulfilled leaders don't leave their growth to chance. They seek accountability, strategic guidance, and an outside perspective to clearly navigate challenges. And that's exactly where executive coaching becomes a game-changer.

Great Leaders Don't Grow in Isolation

Even the highest-performing leaders need guidance. Just like elite athletes work with trainers to refine their skills, leaders need strategic partners who help them align whole-self well-being with professional success.

An executive coach isn't just a sounding board—they're an accelerator.

What a Strong Executive Coach Can Do for You:

- Expose blind spots: Because the biggest barriers to success are the ones you don't see.

- Provide clarity in challenges: So you make smarter, faster decisions under pressure.

- Hold you accountable: Ensuring you build sustainable habits that actually move the needle.

- Align personal and professional growth: Helping you succeed without sacrificing well-being.

AI tools can track progress and suggest action steps but can't replace human connection. A great coach pushes you when you need it, holds you accountable when you waver, and challenges you to step fully into your potential.

Audacious Act #5: Invest in Your Future—Hire an Executive Coach

The boldest leaders don't wait until they're overwhelmed to seek support—they invest in it before they need it.

Take the leap if you're serious about leading with clarity, building an intentional legacy, and sustaining peak performance without burnout. Hire a coach. Commit to your growth. Surround yourself with people who make you better.

The best leaders don't go it alone—and neither should you.

Intentional Resource Allocation: Invest in What Matters

How you allocate your time, energy, and resources doesn't just define what you achieve—it shapes who you become.

Leadership is relentless. You're chasing growth, scaling businesses, and hitting ambitious goals. But if you're not actively deciding where your energy goes, someone else is deciding for you. What if you approached your personal time with the same strategic precision you apply to your business?

Your investments—whether in relationships, well-being, or professional growth—signal your values to the world. Every meeting you take, every project you greenlight, and every hour you spend is a vote for the type of leader you are becoming. The question is: Do your choices align with the impact you want to leave behind?

Leadership is a Ripple Effect

Leaders who intentionally allocate their resources create a ripple effect that extends far beyond themselves.

- When you mentor emerging leaders, you multiply your impact.
- When you support ethical businesses, you set a new standard.
- When you champion initiatives that matter, you shape industries.

According to the American Psychological Association, 73% of employees feel their organization supports a healthy lifestyle when senior leaders model well-being. Your actions don't just define your success—they give others permission to lead with purpose.

Legacy Isn't Built by Chance

The leaders you admire—whether in business, philanthropy, or social change—didn't make an impact by accident.

They made bold, intentional choices that shaped their success and the success of those around them. What is the most audacious thing you can do as a leader? Take full ownership of how you invest your time, talents, and influence.

Audacious Act #6: Make a Legacy Investment Today

Choose one tangible way today to invest in your legacy right now:

- *Mentor a rising leader.*
- *Fund a cause that aligns with your values.*
- *Restructure your calendar to prioritize deep personal work.*
- *Say no to obligations that don't serve your mission so you can serve your well-being.*

Legacy isn't built in the distant future. It's created moment by moment, decision by decision.

Take action today that your future self—and the people you impact—will thank you for.

Go Forth, Audacious One!

Leadership isn't just about achieving success—it's about creating something that lasts. Legacy isn't built in a single moment; it's shaped by the daily choices you make to lead with intention, energy, and alignment.

By committing to the six audacious acts, you're not just supporting your legacy—you're redefining leadership itself. Naming what matters, seeking radical feedback, reclaiming your sense of self, making peace with disappointing others, investing in your own growth, and making daily legacy investments aren't just strategies—they are bold declarations that leadership and well-being are not separate pursuits, but powerful forces that amplify one another.

True impact comes from the leaders who prioritize their well-being, protect their energy, and take ownership of their time, decisions, and influence. When you lead audaciously, you don't just thrive—you empower those around you to do the same.

So, step forward with clarity. Own your energy. Build your legacy. Lead audaciously. The future of leadership starts with the choices you make today.

***

To contact Stevi:

www.stevi.me

Subscribe to our newsletter: www.wisewellnessguild.com

Work with WISe: www.wisewellnessguildpartners.com

Let's connect: stevi@wisewellnessguild.com

Follow me on social media: @stevi.me, @wise_wellness_guild

Connect on LinkedIn: www.linkedin.com/in/stevi-gable-carr

513.503.2989

Huong Nguyen

Huong Nguyen is an Investment and Elite Mindset Coach, Motivational Speaker, Investor, Entrepreneur, Tony Robbins Platinum Partner. She has appeared on Vietnam Television for happiness and other programs, been in newspapers, and organized hundreds of training programs through her own academy. Her work has helped thousands of people heal their past trauma, unlock their abundance mindset, define their own success and happiness, and live their best lives.

Her favorite quote is: **Success isn't about what you get, it's about who you become.**

Huong has always been curious and passionate about life and has never stopped learning and growing. She started working early at 16, was employed by MNCs, opened different businesses, invested in real estate- positioned herself as a "Cashflow Queen," traveled the world, studying from the world classed mentors. She had chances to meet and work with many successful people, but at the end of the day, she found out that many are struggling with emotional life, trying to look rich outside, but broken inside. *"Some have everything but not themselves"*, she said.

Her brand name is Happynow, and the slogan " Happynow is abundance now" means wealth and success are *states of mind first*. If you believe, *"I'll be happy when I am successful, or I'll be happy when I have money,"* you'll always chase it. But if you believe, *"I am already abundant, and money is coming to me,"* then wealth becomes a natural extension of who you are.

Success with peace of mind – Building wealth in JOY Where achievement is harmoniously aligned with inner peace and happiness.

By Huong Nguyen

What does success mean to you? Are you chasing success or attracting success?

Success isn't about *what* you get, it's about *who* you become.

"Set a goal to become a millionaire not for the money, but for the person you'll have to become to achieve it.", Jim Rohn. The wealth, the freedom, the lifestyle… they are just byproducts of your growth. If you chase money without evolving, it won't last. But if you *become* the person who naturally attracts success, it's inevitable.

The investment Legend, Warren Buffet has got a brilliant definition of success: *I measure of Success by how many people love me*. Unlike traditional views that equate success with wealth, status, or achievements, Buffett emphasizes the importance of meaningful relationships and the impact we have on others.

<u>Thought corner: Who are you choosing to become and why?</u>

Why Becoming is More Crucial Than Getting?

1. You Attract What You Are, Not What You Want.

You attract what you are, not what you want, because life reflects your energy, mindset, and actions rather than just your desires. If you seek wealth, success, or love, you must first embody those qualities yourself. Simply wanting something is not enough; your thoughts, behaviors, beliefs and actions shape the reality you create. For example, a person who radiates confidence and kindness is more likely to attract supportive and loving relationships than someone who merely wishes for them but harbors negativity or self-doubt. By focusing on self-growth and becoming the best version of yourself, you naturally draw in experiences and people that align with your energy.

2. Getting Without Growth is Temporary

Lottery winners who don't develop a wealth mindset then lose it all. Lottery winners who don't develop a wealth mindset often lose it all because they never became the kind of person who knows how to build, manage, and sustain wealth. They receive a sudden windfall but still think, spend, and act like they did before leading to reckless spending, poor investments, and financial instability. Without the habits of budgeting, investing, and growing money, their wealth fades as quickly as it came. True financial success isn't about how much money you get—it's about who you become in the process. Without the right mindset, even millions can disappear. But with it, wealth can grow and last for generations.

Entrepreneurs who grow into millionaires, billionaires keep building more wealth because they became that person. Entrepreneurs who grow into millionaires don't just accumulate wealth—they transform into the kind of person who naturally attracts and multiplies it. Through experience, discipline, and mindset shifts, they develop the habits, skills, and thinking patterns that make wealth-building second nature. They see opportunities where others see obstacles, make strategic decisions with a long-term vision, and continuously invest in growth—both personal and financial. Even if they lost everything, they would rebuild because their wealth isn't just in their bank accounts—it's in who they have become.

I suggest some new beliefs to install for your mindset:

- *I focus on becoming a person of value, and success follows.*
- *Every challenge is shaping me into the strongest version of myself.*
- *I don't just chase money, I become the kind of person who naturally attracts it.*
- *I don't chase love- I become Love, and Love comes to me naturally.*

When you shift your focus to who you are becoming, the results will take care of themselves.

3. The Journey is the Real Reward

Success with peace of mind means that happiness is real when it is here and now, not something delayed for the future. When you learn to enjoy the journey, embrace growth, and find fulfillment in the present, you create a success that is both lasting and deeply rewarding.

The Wrong Approach:

- *"I'll be happy when... I make $1 million."*
- *"I'll feel successful when... I get my dream job."*
- *"I'll be complete when... I find the right relationship."*

These beliefs create a happiness trap—you keep pushing happiness into the future, and when you achieve the goal, you just do not feel happy anymore because you start worrying looking for another goal. Run you RACE but make sure you enjoy the VIEW!

The Right Approach:

- *"I enjoy the process of becoming wealthy."*
- *"I love the challenge of growing in my career."*
- *"I am whole now, and my relationships add to my joy."*

Why Happiness Leads to Success?

A lot of people think success equals happiness, but the truth is often the opposite:

Happiness creates success. When you start from happiness, you perform better, think clearer, and attract more opportunities. Here's why:

1. **Studies show that happy people perform better at work and in life.** In the book: The Happiness Advantage by Shawn Achor: In his groundbreaking book, Achor, a researcher and positive psychology expert, shares his research showing that happier people are more productive, creative, and resilient. One of his studies found that employees who were shown positive, uplifting content before performing tasks were more likely to perform better and demonstrate higher levels of creativity than those who weren't given

such priming. Happiness, he argues, fuels success rather than being a result of it.

The Broaden-and-Build Theory by Barbara Fredrickson: Fredrickson's research on positive emotions supports the idea that happiness broadens our cognitive and emotional scope, allowing for more creative thinking, better problem-solving, and stronger relationships. She argues that positive emotions, like happiness, enable people to build personal resources (social, intellectual, and physical), which in turn improves their ability to perform well in both professional and personal life.

2. **Happiness attracts opportunities.**

People love being around positive, energized individuals. Happiness fosters authentic connections with others. People are naturally drawn to those who radiate positivity, making it more likely that you'll find supportive mentors, collaborators, or even career opportunities simply because others enjoy being around you. Your enthusiasm and confidence also inspire trust, making others more willing to offer you opportunities.

3. **A happy mindset makes you resilient.**

You bounce back faster from failures and keep moving forward. When you're positive, you're less likely to become overwhelmed by adversity, and you can maintain clarity of thought even in tough circumstances. This emotional stability allows you to stay calm, make better decisions, and persevere in the face of challenges. Additionally, happiness boosts your physical and mental health, further supporting your ability to stay strong and recover quickly from hardships.

Happy people bounce back faster because they have emotional strength and perspective.

Joy helps you stay in the game—and wealth favors those who stay.

4. **Happy people take more actions**.

Because you feel good NOW, you are motivated to catch your dreams. Happy people are often more motivated and driven to take actions because their positive mindset fuels their energy and enthusiasm. When you're happy, you're more likely to feel confident, optimistic, and capable of handling challenges, which encourages you to take proactive steps toward your goals.

Embracing happiness in a wealth journey allows you to navigate life's challenges with resilience and optimism, which in turn opens doors to new opportunities and experiences. By prioritizing happiness in the present, you are also setting the stage for a fulfilling and successful life that's grounded in positivity and authenticity.

The more you invest in enriching your soul, the more abundant and fulfilling your life becomes.

Experiences that enrich your soul, like learning new things, traveling, connecting deeply with others, or pursuing passions, provide long-term fulfillment. These are the things that give you a sense of purpose and lasting joy, which no amount of money can buy.

Travel doesn't just enrich you with new sights and adventures; it broadens your perspective, opens your mind to different cultures, and helps you grow emotionally and intellectually. The knowledge, memories, and connections you gain while traveling are priceless. Every new place you visit adds depth to your understanding of the world and your place within it. Whether through meeting new people, encountering diverse ways of life, or simply stepping outside of your comfort zone, travel enriches your life in ways that accumulate over time. The more you travel, the more you invest in your personal wealth—wealth that comes from the stories you gather, the lessons you learn, and the ways in which your heart and mind expand.

Wealth, in this sense, is about cultivating a rich inner life—one that radiates positivity, contentment, and resilience. It's about finding meaning in everyday moments and aligning your actions with your values.

The Importance of Having an Investment Coach/ Life Coach

A coach is not a luxury nor an expense- it is a profitable investment—it's a necessity if you want to accelerate your success, avoid costly mistakes, and reach your full potential. Even the most successful people—top CEOs, world-class athletes, and billionaires—have coaches to guide them.

A life coach/ investment coach is a game-changer on your journey to greatness. Whether in personal development or wealth-building, having the right mentor shortens your learning curve, keeps you accountable, and helps you achieve results faster.

Building wealth in Joy: How to feel better when bad things happen?

A winning mindset helps you through when circumstances are challenging.

5 ways to help your mind work FOR you, not against you

- Give your brain a project - Spend 15 minutes working on a project that matters to you. Organize a closet, jump into a good book, learn a language, or pick up an instrument; creativity can pull you out of negativity.

- Use manifestation: Dr. James Doty, a neurosurgeon and neuroscientist, says there are five steps to manifest:

    > Choose a thought you want to live by and follow these steps: (1). Write it down (2). Read it silently (3). Read it aloud (4). Visualize (5). Repeat over and over again.

    This process calibrates the brain's Default Mode Network, replacing self-doubt and negative thought loops with the empowerment you need.

- Start your day with a sentence: Psychiatrist and brain expert Dr. Daniel Amen starts every morning by saying, "Today is going to be a great day."

    Starting your day this way immediately puts your mind in a positive state and directs the Reticular Activating System, the brain filter, to find evidence to make it so. "The brain is lazy. It does what you nudge it to do," he says.

- Quiet your mind- Mindfulness is not about stopping thoughts; it is about observing them without attachment. Notice them; do not grip them.

Imagine your thoughts floating away like leaves down a river. Let them rise and fall. Studies show that detaching from negative thoughts reduces stress and rewires your brain for positivity.

- Develop Positive Incantations: Use Incantations to build a mindset that supports your goals and values. Remind yourself daily of your strengths, capabilities, and purpose. Positive self-talk rewires your brain, reinforcing a mindset of self-belief and empowerment.

II. The Awakened Millionaire: The Power of Conscious Wealth Creation

The concept of the **Awakened Millionaire** represents a shift in how we perceive success and wealth. In the past, accumulating wealth was often viewed as the ultimate goal, regardless of the personal or social costs. Today, however, a growing number of successful individuals are embracing the idea that true abundance goes beyond financial prosperity. The awakened millionaire achieves financial success while aligning their life with a sense of **purpose, mindfulness, and social responsibility**.

Awakened Millionaire is about breaking free from traditional models of wealth creation that focus solely on material accumulation. Instead, it is a movement toward creating wealth that is in harmony with one's values, a deeper sense of self-awareness, and a desire to positively impact the world. The awakened millionaire knows that wealth is not just about what you earn but also about how you live, the relationships you build, and the legacy you create.

7 ways to become an Awakened Millionaire

1. Cultivate Self-Awareness and Purpose

- The first step to becoming an awakened millionaire is **developing a strong sense of self-awareness**. Understand what truly matters to you, your values, passions, and life purpose. Wealth should be a tool to amplify your purpose, not just a personal goal. When you're clear on your purpose, you can align your financial efforts with what you truly want to contribute to the world.

2. Mindful Decision-Making

- Awakened millionaires don't make decisions impulsively or out of fear. Instead, they practice **mindfulness** to make deliberate, thoughtful choices that serve their goals and values. Whether it's a business move, investment, or personal relationship, they take the time to reflect, consider long-term impacts, and act with intention.

4. Practice Gratitude and Abundance

- Developing an **abundance mindset** is key. Instead of seeing wealth as a finite resource, awakened millionaires embrace the belief that there is always more to go around. They practice gratitude for the wealth they have and are open to receiving more. Gratitude shifts the focus from lack to plenty, helping you attract more opportunities, wealth, and success.

5. Prioritize Inner Peace and Emotional Balance

- The pursuit of wealth can often bring stress, anxiety, and burnout. An awakened millionaire places a high priority on **inner peace, emotional well-being, and balance**. They incorporate practices like meditation, yoga, journaling, and self-reflection to maintain mental clarity and emotional resilience.

6. Focus on Long-Term Legacy

- Instead of focusing solely on short-term profits, the awakened millionaire thinks about their **legacy**—the impact they will leave behind. This includes how they treat others, what they contribute to their community, and the lessons they pass down. Building a lasting legacy is more important than fleeting success.

7. Surround Yourself with Like-minded People

- Being an awakened millionaire doesn't mean doing it alone. Surround yourself with people who share your vision for conscious wealth-building and personal growth. Engage with mentors, peers, and communities that encourage both financial success and personal evolution.

I am creating an Awaken Millionaire Club, whether you are already Billionaires, Millionaires or not; if you are interested, drop me an email at **huong.happy84@gmail.com** *and your details. We will qualify before adding you to the peer group. I am thankful you are reading until here. Hope to welcome you on board, my new friends, my Awakened Millionaires!*

III. Wealth, Love & Happiness: The Ultimate Power Couple Journey

Building a harmonious and passionate relationship and wealth at the same time is not only possible but also deeply rewarding. A successful partnership, where both individuals support each other's goals, can create a solid foundation for achieving financial prosperity. In my career, I have witnessed so many dreams being killed just because the partner is not on the same page. Differences in value and purpose can be the fastest way to end our wealth in joy. I believe choosing the right partner 80% determines your wealth. Here's how you can nurture both aspects simultaneously:

1. Shared Vision and Goals

A harmonious relationship thrives on clear communication and shared values. When it comes to building wealth, it's essential that both partners are on the same page. Discuss your financial goals, whether it's buying a home, saving for retirement, or investing in a business. By aligning your objectives and expectations, you create a powerful team that works together toward financial success.

2. Effective Communication

Open and honest communication is the cornerstone of any successful relationship. Wealth-building means discussing money openly, setting a budget, and deciding where to allocate resources.

When both partners are involved in financial planning, it prevents misunderstandings and fosters a sense of shared responsibility.

3. Mutual Support and Encouragement

Building wealth often comes with setbacks and challenges. In a harmonious relationship, partners support each other through tough times and celebrate victories. Whether encouraging each other to pursue career advancements, start a side business, or learn new financial skills, mutual support strengthens both the relationship and wealth-building efforts.

4. Balancing Personal Growth and Collective Goals

Both individuals need space to grow individually while nurturing their collective goals. Encouraging each other's professional development while also investing time in the relationship creates a balanced and supportive environment. This allows both partners to thrive both personally and financially, ultimately contributing to long-term happiness and wealth.

5. Wealth Beyond Money

Building wealth isn't only about finances. A harmonious relationship creates emotional wealth through trust, respect, and love, contributing to long-term happiness. When a couple feels emotionally fulfilled, they have the mental clarity and energy needed to focus on achieving financial goals together.

6. Planning for the Future Together

Establishing financial security for future retirement planning, saving for children's education, or buying insurance—requires teamwork and long-term vision. These conversations strengthen the relationship, ensuring both partners feel confident and secure in their financial future.

7. Invest in couple therapist, investment coach, financial planner services

Working with a trusted financial expert, you can gain clarity, reduce financial stress, and create a roadmap for lasting financial success.

Likewise, investing in a couple therapist is like investing in wealth—both require time, effort, and commitment, but the returns can be life-changing. Just as financial investments secure a stable future, therapy strengthens the foundation of a relationship, preventing emotional "bankruptcy" caused by unresolved conflicts, poor communication, or trust issues.

A strong relationship is an asset, impacting mental well-being, personal growth, and even professional success. When partners work through challenges together, they create a healthier, more supportive environment that fosters happiness and stability. Just as financial wealth provides security and opportunities, emotional wealth—built through therapy—ensures a fulfilling and lasting connection.

Ultimately, a harmonious relationship and wealth-building are interconnected. When partners work together with trust, clear communication, shared goals, they create a stronger foundation for both emotional fulfillment and financial success. By prioritizing both personal and collective growth, couples can enjoy the journey of building a life of abundance—both in love and in wealth. I wish both of you live with passion and enjoy this journey to the fullest!

***

Contact:

Email: Huong.happy84@gmail.com,

Instagram: HuongNguyen_HappyNow

Facebook: Huong Nguyen

LinkedIn: Huong Nguyen

Michelle Mueller Ihrig

Michelle Mueller Ihrig is passionate about inspiring connection for individual, organizational and planetary wellbeing. She is a multipotentialite- leading and working in hospitality, large-scale food service, learning and development and previously global relocations. Michelle is a coach, facilitator and international speaker. A global citizen, her journey spans the Côte d'Ivoire, Canada, Germany, Vietnam, and Thailand.

She founded MC^2 leadership coaching, rooted in her values of being Mindful, Curious, and Connected. It reflects the natural law of energy, where cause and effect create an environmental ripple. We all lead when we choose, and it starts from our heart.

A founding member of Flourish3 coaching collective, Michelle leads workshops and retreats in mindfulness, mindset and awareness, reinstating our mind-body connection in elevating our best selves.

Michelle has spoken at the Stanford Women's Leadership Summit, the Women Empowerment Conference in Paris, and to the D1 Lindenwood Rugby Team on unleashing potential through mindfulness. She served as a council member at Stanford's Women Leadership Development Program, and as an instructor at the Healthy Living Program.

An ICF-certified coach, NLP-certified practitioner, Pranayama facilitator, 3 Brains Intelligence Coach, and the Connection Practice Coach and Trainer, Michelle empowers individuals and teams to lead with alignment and grounded purpose to impact positive change.

Navigating by Heart

By Michelle Ihrig

'The longest journey in life is the one foot from your head to your heart.'

(Native American Proverb)

'I'm lost,' said the head. 'The map is right inside your chest,' whispered the heart. 'I can't hear your direction,' replied the head, 'Take a moment to pause, be still and focus. Then you'll hear my guidance,' affirmed the heart.

Do you sometimes feel lost, searching outside yourself for the answers? Have you ever asked yourself, where am I in connection to myself, my relationships, my work, my impact? The answer lies in our ability to align our heads with the calm, rhythmic guide of our hearts in finding clarity, ease, and direction. Navigating by heart operates from a grounded center versus external reactionary mode. By tapping into our higher selves, we can lead our lives with more thoughtful intention, connection, and well-being while also realizing our true individual and collective influence in the world.

While taking a CPR class a few years ago, I was absolutely stunned by something the instructor said, 'You can die from a broken heart.' What? That statement struck a chord deep inside me. It confirmed what I had always sensed: that our mind, heart, and body relationship is much more powerful than we ever knew.

Our bodies are fascinating sources of wisdom. It is amazing what we can learn when we listen to them. Like the natural world around us, the human body is an ecosystem working around the clock to create a state of harmony and balance. When something becomes off balance, our body signals us with a sensation or a feeling. Our body is constantly communicating with us, but are we listening? Ancestral cultures understood this and lived in a deeper state of connection, operating in sync with their body as a directional life force.

In today's modern world, there is so much external noise and distraction that we get stuck in our heads, making it hard to hear our own voice. We become lost as our compass navigates on external stimuli. Faced with relentless messages of scarcity, conflict, and worthlessness, our sympathetic nervous system remains in a state of 'fight or flight mode' as we sense danger all around. While we're naturally wired to be on the lookout for danger, the challenge today is the sheer speed at which negative information spreads and is consumed, blurring the line between real and perceived threats. Our head spins away with fear, doubt, and confusion. The power of the heart reigns the mind back in, with intentional focus guiding us to a state of connection and balance.

Powered by Heart

The heart produces the largest electromagnetic field in the body and is the key force that influences the brain. *In fact, about 90% of information flows from the heart to the brain —bottom-up, not top-down, as we once thought.* When our heart is stressed, it signals the brain to reinforce feelings of tension and anxiety. When we focus on calming techniques like deep breathing, our heart sends signals through the vagus nerve that help activate the parasympathetic nervous system—the body's natural 'calm mode.' Hormones are released that promote relaxation and ease.

The HeartMath Institute, a leading research organization on the heart-brain connection, calls this heart coherence - "a highly efficient state in which all the body's systems work together in harmony. Increasing personal coherence creates an alignment of mind, body, emotions and spirit through the power of the heart."

Heart coherence enhances our emotional intelligence and widens the gap between stimulus and response. It gives us greater agency and allows us to have improved relationships with ourselves and others. A calm nervous system reduces stress and inflammation, which promotes both our mental and physical well-being. It grows our resilience and the ability to bounce forward after inevitable setbacks in life. Coherence fosters creativity, which taps into our higher thinking, improving decision-making and mental clarity. It nurtures self-trust and confidence. Essentially, it brings out the best in us, navigating life with more grounded ease and direction.

One of my favorite quotes is from Dr. Viktor Frankl, a holocaust survivor, who said, 'Between stimulus and response there is a space. In that space is our power to choose our response. In our response lies our growth and our freedom.' While we have little control over external events, we can choose to focus on what we can control - our own response and how we choose to show up. Through mindfulness practices, we can generate heart coherence within ourselves while also positively impacting our surroundings at the same time.

Electromagnetic Field of Influence

Incredibly, the electromagnetic field of our heart can be measured up to several feet outside ourselves. Our heart's powerful rhythm can sync with and influence the heartbeat and energy of those around us. Ever thought you don't have much influence on those around you? You do.

The heart is the body's largest built-in rhythm generator. A concept from physics called *entrainment* explains how rhythmic systems synchronize with the strongest one. The heart's dominant rhythm has the power to align the mind and body back into balance. A simple example of this is when you place grandfather clocks of different sizes in the same room. Initially, their pendulums swing at different speeds, but over time, they begin to sync up with the rhythm of the strongest.

Think about the last time you entered a meeting room or a coffee shop and immediately felt welcome or unwelcome. This is your heart detecting the energetic state of others. As the saying goes, don't adapt to the energy in the room, be the energy in the room. I enjoy being intentional with grounded interactions and adopting a proactive approach, smiling and making eye contact when greeting others, being curious and asking questions, standing tall with open body language, and speaking with engaging respect. As you bring purposeful, heart-centered energy to any interaction, a sense of expansiveness and empowerment grows.

This energetic influence extends beyond ourselves; it's being measured on a global scale. HeartMath's Global Coherence Initiative is an effort that has placed six magnetometers across the globe to observe changes in the earth's magnetic field and how it is impacted by human emotion and behaviors. The findings show that when people come together with attitudes of love, appreciation, and care, this has a positive global impact. The influential ripple effect of our own and collective well-being is real. It proves the interconnectedness that binds all things, including the natural world around us.

While in Thailand, I met survivors of the devastating 2002 tsunami. One couple shared that they were sitting on the beach observing a line of ants running busily up and down the sides of a table in the sand. Suddenly, all the ants disappeared. Minutes later, the ocean water line started to recede at an unusual rate. The couple acted on their awareness and left the beach. Other survivors witnessed animals such as dogs and elephants leave the coastal areas at the same time. While I am not a scientist, it appears that their inner navigation system detected the change in the electromagnetic field based on a geographical shift in energy. While this example goes beyond what happens with the human heart's energetic exchange, it highlights the power of feeling through our heart, rather than simply relying on the intellect of our head to guide us.

Mindfulness Practices for Everyday - Out of our Head and into our Heart

Mindfulness techniques are the way to connect to the grounding guidance of our hearts. Simply put, mindfulness is focused attention and raised awareness. With the awareness of our mind being hijacked by external stimuli into stress and autopilot, we can choose to redirect our attention by taking a focused pause that brings us back to the present.

While I love many mindfulness practices, below are seven of my favorites, serving as a reset button that can be incorporated into your daily routine. Each one has an immediate positive effect. Like a muscle, you will notice a heart-centered approach strengthens over time. Enjoy trying the different practices and notice how they resonate.

Awe

Awe connects us to something larger than ourselves and reveals the extraordinary in the ordinary. Awe sensations arise as your vagus nerve is activated and oxytocin is released. Einstein said awe is the most human emotion vital to flourishing; it opens our hearts and minds to a new sense of wonder and perspective.

I'll never forget my first real experience with awe as a child living in Venezuela. My family frequented a place called Isla Larga (meaning 'large island,' yet funny enough, this is the smallest island I have ever visited). A shipwreck lay submerged beneath the water, its rusted frame intact on the ocean floor, creating the perfect snorkeling spot. As I swam through the crystal clear waters, gliding over the ship's eerie silhouette, the ocean floor began to disappear into the dark blue abyss. The wrecks of the ship were only partially visible yet were surrounded by the most colorful ocean life I have ever seen. It was still yet teeming with life in waters of immense and vast presence, terrifying and awe-striking at the same time. As soon as I left the water, there was no such sign of the other world that existed just beneath. It was an unforgettable awakening to something much larger than me.

Thankfully, we don't need to snorkel at a shipwreck to experience awe. It's around us everywhere, waiting to be noticed when we pause and get curious.

Curiosity

Returning to the US in July 2020 amidst the height of the pandemic after living abroad for 20 years was daunting. With no job lined up, I was faced with an overwhelming sense of uncertainty and fear. A senior partner at a leadership consultancy gave me one piece of advice: always remain curious. Curious about your situation, what there is to learn, of the world around you. Curiosity is a source of inspiration, growth, and expansion. It increases knowledge and confidence. I became very curious when I heard trees talk to one another. I learned that beneath the ground on which we walk lies an intricate webbed communication system of roots and organisms sending informative signals and nutrients to one another to support their interdependent thriving. They warn each other of threats such as drought or insect attacks, with the oldest trees storing the most information. Even the smallest fungi play a vital role in this exchange. Some people call this system the internet of nature, the 'wood wide web.' It brought me back to awe right outside my front door. What would it look like for you to adopt a mindset of curiosity? What can you become curious about in your immediate surroundings or from challenging situations in your life? What do they teach you?

Meditation

Meditation can take many forms. I used to think one had to sit still and clear one's mind of any thoughts, but I quickly abandoned that method as it didn't work for me. Years later, I returned to it, having discovered guided meditations, either in person or on an App. Listening to a daily guided meditation on an app has become part of my morning routine and sets a grounded tone for my day.

Meditation can also be used to radiate positive energy bubbles on others, called metta meditation. Use the phrases: may you be happy, may you be healthy, may you be at ease, may you be safe; intentionally walk past others and wish this silently upon them, witnessing your own mood and the vibe around shift. The effects can be magnified when done in collaboration with others as you walk along together!

Movement

If there is anything to do daily, it's to move our bodies. We were born to move, something our modern sedentary lifestyle works against. Movement allows emotions and feelings to move through and acts as a natural energizer- literally getting unstuck and into a state of flow. Nine out of ten times, ideas or problems I had been ruminating on, including writing the chapter for this book, became clear as soon as I started to move, especially when outside.

3 Ways to Move

Dance: Turn on some music and dance around! Have some fun. You'll be amazed at how good this feels. Dancing is a great way to grow trust, confidence, and appreciation for yourself.

Stretch: Roll your head, stretch your arms, twist. Take regular pauses in the day to stretch wherever you are. Share the joy at work and gather your teams for a 5-minute Flex n Stretch for some team building. Stretching with my team became part of my legacy, promoting engagement and well-being. Having cleared our minds and been put at ease, we often came up with great ideas on challenges we faced or innovations for improvements.

Walk: Walking is our body's most natural yet underutilized form of movement. Take time to walk, whether in nature, around the block, by parking further away from your destination, or using the stairs instead of the elevator. Make walking your default and notice your energy and strength increase.

Haiku

A fun practice learned in middle school was recently brought back to my attention during a resilience course. Using this activity in a workshop of mine, a participant from Japan mentioned that their senior communities write haikus as a daily activity to combat Alzheimer's disease. Haikus also remind us that we are all creative, which is an essential aspect of problem-solving and decision-making. A haiku is a 3-line poem with 17 syllables arranged in a five – seven – five order, typically describing a scene in nature, but it can be anything you feel or see at the time. Let the descriptive words flow without thought and give yourself no more than 1 minute. The syllables can be counted out and edited after. One woman I know carries a small notebook and spontaneously writes a haiku daily.

Gratitude

Pausing to step out of autopilot and take note of something to be grateful in the moment is tremendously grounding. Keep a journal or take a mental or verbal note of three things that naturally come to mind. Then, think of three more from your everyday life that are often overlooked and taken for granted. For me, the easiest examples of gratitude are family, healthy food, and home. When I look deeper, three more include clean drinking water, clean air, and physical health. Gratitude practices are great to incorporate into a morning or bedtime routine. They are also a fantastic team-building tool, as an ice breaker for starting or ending a meeting. How do you feel when you start noticing the things to be grateful for in your life?

Breath

Breath is our life force. It is the first thing we do when we are born; it's the last thing we do before we die. It's our most powerful resource for well-being. It immediately impacts our parasympathetic nervous system through the regulation of heart rate and brings calm as we focus and slow the breathing. When stressed, our breathing tends to be fast and shallow, further exasperating our state of being and depleting us of vital oxygen. With simple awareness, we can take focused breaths and ignite our relaxation response.

Breathing is a constant exchange of giving and receiving. We receive vital oxygen and exhale carbon dioxide, releasing what we don't need. Trees and plants around us receive carbon dioxide as their vital source and release oxygen. We are engaging in the perfect interconnectedness of all things, serving as a reminder of why nature is so important for our health and well-being as we physically rely on one another.

3 Ways to Breathe

Sigh: Sighing is a natural stress relief response that happens automatically. Sighing with intention includes noticing when it could benefit you, breathing deeply through the nose, and making an audible exhale through the mouth. If at work or surrounded by others, exhaling through the nose is also highly impactful.

Balloon Breathing: Close your eyes and breathe deeply as you allow your stomach to expand like a balloon to the count of 4. Slowly exhale for the count of 4 while pushing the navel back towards the spine. Hold your breath at the tip of each inhale and exhale. Repeat this several times. For maximum benefit, the exhalation can be slightly longer than the count of 6.

Anulom Vilom- is a pranayama practice of alternate nose breathing. Putting the thumb and middle finger on opposite sides of the nose, close the right nostril first and breathe in through the left for a count of 4, close both nostrils and hold the breath for a count of 4, release the right nostril and exhale right for the count of 6. Inhale right for 4, hold the breath for 4, exhale left for 6. Continue the alternate pattern for a few minutes, ending with an exhale on the left nostril.

Navigating by Heart

Through mindfulness, we realize the one-foot journey between our head and our heart becomes a more accessible distance—a bridge we learn to cross by tuning in.

Leaving the CPR class that day, I was clear in my resolve to tend to my own heart. Understanding the true power of the heart as the driver of our well-being, connection, and influencing capacities for positive change around us gave me a greater incentive to nourish trust, safety, and expansion within myself. What would it look like to live in a world where more of us navigated by heart? Our heart is responsible for love, community and belonging. It is bold, fierce, and courageous, with a deep wisdom of our interconnectedness. While we cannot control the storm, we can choose to go to the calm eye of the hurricane and tap into our inner strength. Understanding that energetic presence is real and comes from bottom up, inside out, imagine the limitless power of you. Hope, compassion and action are contagious, empowering teams and communities. To meet the rising global challenges of today, supporting our best selves through the intentional guide of our hearts is essential. It's time to go beyond the noise and step into the powerful impact of navigating by heart.

**

To contact Michelle:

W: MC2leadership.com

E: michelleihrig@me.com

Corey Poirier

Corey Poirier is a (5 x) multiple-time TEDx speaker, SUCCESS Magazine Emerging Entrepreneur and a Wall Street Journal / USA Today Bestselling Author.

He is also the host of the top rated 'Let's Do Influencing' Radio Show, founder of The Speaking Program, founder of bLU Talks, and he has been featured in multiple television specials and he is also a Barnes and Noble, Amazon, Apple Books and Kobo Bestselling Author.

A columnist with Entrepreneur and Forbes magazine, he has featured in/on CBS, CTV, NBC, ABC, CBS, is a Forbes Coaches Council member, and is one of the few leaders featured four times on the popular Entrepreneur on Fire show.

He has also interviewed over 7,500 of the world's top leaders and he has spoken on-site at events Harvard, Stanford, Columbia, UCLA, MIT, Cambridge, UCLA, and Oxford.

The Power of Synchronicity

By Corey Poirier

Do you believe in synchronicity?

At one time I didn't – today, I'm a firm believer. I'm sold.

Let me give you an example of a really cool Synchronicity that happened not so long ago.

I was speaking at an event in Western Canada.

A lady at the event approached me afterward, and we had a great conversation.

I didn't know where the conversation may lead but was simply happy to have a great conversation on a Saturday after speaking (my passion) on a subject I'm super passionate about (writing).

Shortly after the conversation, the lady introduced me to her son, Kent.

Kent is the founder of TV Network. I had known of the network previous to meeting Kent, but then I dived in further.

The network is a great platform with many world class shows.

I still didn't know where the connection would lead.

BUT now, I do.

That Network is one of the main official homes of our bLU Talks brand.

This, to me, is a classic example of synchronicity in action. Imagine if Kent's Mother didn't reach out and start a conversation – the rest likely wouldn't have happened.

But she did, and it did. This put our brand on same network that has show's featuring influencers like Jay Shetty and Shaman Durek.

This is just one example of Synchronicity in action…and a real outcome.

Let me give you another.

Years ago I had a reading by a psychic.

You may not believe in psychic mediums.

I certainly didn't for the first half of my life.

The psychic in question, her name was Sue. We have since started calling her Oracle Sue.

Well, during the reading she told me I would meet someone soon with Prominent L's in their name.

I figured it was the first letter of their first name and first letter of their last name that was start with an L.

That is until I met Shelley. Shelley of course has two L's in her name.

Now with things like this, you can simply say, well, you're reaching to say L's meant Shelley, and maybe you just acted when you met someone with L's in their name.

I would tend to agree.

However, it gets deeper.

Sue told me that after I met L, my life would change dramatically, and I would end up working with an Author in the Southern States that would open many doors.

She also said that she saw L and I on Horseback in Sedona, Arizona at sunset.

I had never heard of Sedona, and I asked her what Sedona was.

Ultimately, after the reading, I ended up connecting with someone who grew up in the same town I had.

Her name was of course Shelley.

In short, over the course of a few months, we ended up dating.

Not long after that we drove across the US and Canada together and for my 40th birthday she bought me horseback riding lessons in Sedona.

She didn't know about Oracle Sue's prediction.

It gets better (and deeper).

About a year into my relationship with Shelley, I asked her if she wanted me to interview any big name thought leaders she was a fan of.

She mentioned a spiritual author who had heavily impacted her life.

I started to see how I could reach him.

With big names like his, it's very rare to find a way to contact them on their website, or it's typically a form or info at type email and sadly, most times you don't receive a reply.

I was shocked to find his personal email address on the website.

I emailed him and explained the situation.

A few weeks later I heard back from someone on his team that he would be happy to do an interview.

Oh, and interestingly he only put his email address on the website for 3 weeks, the same 3 weeks I visited his website for how to contact him. He took it down shortly after because he became flooded with emails.

To save you the details, he and I built a relationship, and I ended up interviewing him many times before he asked me to come to his place and stay in the same cabin where his mega bestselling book was written.

While there we discussed working on a documentary together about his work.

The result was I picked a list of people who I felt would be a great fit in the documentary and I set out to line up interviews.

I ended up traveling and conducting the interviews and meeting some of the biggest names in the personal development field - it opened many doors.

Remember what Oracle Sue said?

You'll meet someone with prominent L's in their name, and you'll end up on Horseback at Sunset in Sedona and also connecting with an Author who will open many new doors. Oh, and he was based in the Southern US as she indicated.

You can't make this stuff up ... but imagine if I didn't act on the chance to connect with Shelley, none of the rest happens.

Here's a 3rd, shorter, synchronicity story – to drive the point home.

While I was doing the interviews for the documentary, I was supposed to meet an interviewee at a location in Miami.

He gave me the wrong address and when we found out, I was already an hour and a half away from his office at the time the interview was supposed to start.

He said he would wait until I got to his office but once I got there, I had a message from him saying, "Sorry, champ, had to bail"

My plan was to simply go to Miami beach to make lemonade out of the lemons I had just been handed.

Before I got to the beach however, I had a text from a friend.

She said, "aren't you in Miami today?"

I said I was.

She said, "remember that guy I told you I thought you should interview from Miami who had moved to a different country? Well, he moved back to Miami if you wanted me to see if he is available while you're there"

I said that would be amazing but also that I was he would busy with this short of notice.

Well, it turned out, that he had two or three meetings cancelled on him that afternoon, which was rare, and he agreed to meet.

After the interview he asked me who else he could introduce me to.

I said I didn't want to take advantage of our new relationship but added that if he thought of anyone to feel free to text me.

By the time I got back to my hotel I had a text from him that said, how about Les Brown and Bob Proctor.

I was a big fan of both Les and Bob, who was still alive at the time, and I agreed that it would be amazing if he could make those connections.

He did, and I had the opportunity to interview Bob before his passing, and to hold and look through his 60+ year old copy of Think and Grow Rich while sitting by his pool, taking the moment in, and I also had the opportunity to interview Les Brown no less than 5 times as well.

Let's go back to the synchronicity idea.

Let's consider the synchronicity of the guy I was supposed to interview sending me to the wrong place, and then my friend texting me about doing an interview the same day in Miami – an interview I wouldn't have been able to do had the first one not cancelled.

Oh, and years later, I did get to interview the guy who sent me the wrong address.

Had the original interview happened though, I would likely never have met Bob Proctor before he passed, and Les Brown so many times since.

I hope when you consider these three stories, and I have ones happening, similar to these ones, every single week now, you can see why I started to believe in the power of synchronicity.

Now, I guess the one question you may ask at this point is, "how do I start bringing similar synchronicities into my life on a regular basis?"

I feel, based on my experience, it comes down to a few simple steps.

- Paying attention when things that may seem like coincidences happen. I believe if you acknowledge them, you will see them more or get more of them. I started writing in a synchronicity journal as a way of noticing and acknowledging them.
- Lean in (or out). When my friend texted me about meeting up with the person in Miami, I recognized it was a meaningful coincidence, and I leaned in and took action. Had I said, nah, I'm heading to the beach now, none of the rest (i.e. interviewing him, Les Brown and Bob Proctor) would have happened.
- Notice when you see people or things happen multiple times and try to determine what message is in that for you. If it's a

person, you could simply start up a conversation and see what you learn.

With that, I truly hope this chapter has offered you some ideas for how you could bring more synchronicities into your life, and how you can take advantage of the power of synchronicity to better your life; and/or even your business.

Until then, here's to your greater success.

***

Contact Info:

www.blutalks.com

www.coreypoiriermedia.com

media@blutalks.com

Marie Zunda

Marie Zunda is a certified transformational life coach (CPCC) and high-performance coach (HPC), dedicated to empowering successful women over 40 to unleash their authentic selves. With a mission to help clients step into their personal power and lead from the heart, Marie guides women to live in alignment with their true essence, fostering lives filled with joy, peace, well-being, success, and fulfillment.

With a Master's in Integrative Health and a Bachelor's from Cornell University, Marie combines deep expertise with a passion for holistic well-being. After a decade in corporate marketing and two decades running a branding design business, she discovered her true calling – helping others transform their lives. A pivotal "broken-open" moment led her to immerse herself in meditation, yoga, positive psychology, and spiritual studies – practices that now form the foundation of her coaching philosophy.

Marie understands the challenges high-achieving women face and provides the tools to help them thrive. Through her company, Ignite Your Best Self, she supports women in transforming their lives from the inside out by empowering them to break free from societal expectations and self-imposed limitations. Her approach integrates mindfulness, self-discovery, and actionable strategies that help women embrace their brilliance.

In addition to coaching, Marie is a teacher and speaker, inspiring women to become the best of who they are. As a devoted mother of two adult children, Marie finds joy in service, lifelong learning, and traveling worldwide.

Soul Reflections to THRIVE

By Marie Zunda

Your soul is a mirror. Look into your soul so you can Rise, Reconnect, and Thrive!

Forward

I'm excited to write a chapter in Cracking the Rich Code, Volume 17 because you can be rich in many ways, including wealth, health, business, relationships, and personal fulfillment. The poet Mary Oliver asks one of my favorite questions *"Tell me, what is it you plan to do with your one wild and precious life?"* We often look outside of ourselves for happiness, but what if you looked inside yourself? What fills you up? What sets your heart on fire? What brings you completely ALIVE? This chapter is about my soul reflections and the wisdom I have learned on my life journey so far. My goal in writing this chapter is to showcase perhaps a new perspective for the reader. Maybe it is something you have never pondered before. There are many opinions and beliefs in this world. I'm not asking for you to agree with me. I believe that we all are sovereign beings and must take new information from outside of ourselves and bring it inside to discern what we believe, whether through our experience, physical proof, or just faith, it matters not. All I ask is that you remain open in a state of "beginner's mind" without judgement or preconceptions. Just bring your curiosity and an open mind. Take what resonates and leave the rest behind. Thank you for going on this inner journey with me.

Chapter

I would like you to ponder the following "What ifs":

- *What if* each human being on this planet has a beautiful light inside, just waiting to shine bright - your soul.
- *What if* your soul came to Earth to learn and grow?
- *What if* you are in the driver's seat of your life and have the power to say YES to yourself and your big dream?

First, let's explore the one thing that connects everyone: the human body. Yes, every human being on this planet has a physical body, which we can see, touch and feel. It is hard to believe that this miracle of creation starts with the meeting of two tiny cells, which then develop into a human being with many organs that know how to keep us alive in each waking moment. Did you know that, on average, a person takes 20,000 breaths daily, moving 10,000 liters of air? Even more astounding, our hearts beat on average 100,000 times a day or 35 million beats a year to keep us alive. What's even crazier is that the human body, with its trillions of cells, undergoes an estimated 37 billion trillion biochemical reactions every second. All of these actions happen without our conscious awareness. I'm sure if we were to look at this process under a microscope in slow motion, it probably looks like a well-timed orchestra that creates each human life form and this beautiful container of a body that also houses our higher mind or ego and lets us think and feel emotions. We truly are multidimensional beings; we think, we feel, we see, we hear, we communicate, we can move, and we have a brain that lets us live and create a life of our own. We are truly a miracle. However, the most important thing that our human body holds safe and sacred is our soul. Our soul, which has come down through the cosmos and landed in a physical body, is the most beautiful. It is the light that is you. Are you letting your soul shine bright?

I believe we are all born with our own gifts and talents. Our soul signature is unique. We have everything we need inside of us to create the life we were meant to live or that our soul contracted to live before we incarnated into this body. You may or may not believe in past lives or karma, but we also come here without a memory of what our soul has experienced in prior lives. Each lifetime is a brand-new, fresh start without a memory or connection to the divine, source, or creator (choose whichever definition you are comfortable with). Many of my teachers over the years have said that "it is a privilege to be in this human body." Apparently, there is a long waitlist to come down to this planet called Earth. It takes some getting used to being in a physical body because, before our incarnation, we, too, were in spirit form, vibrating at the level of the unseen world of guides, guardians, and angels.

So why do we come here to Earth? WHY? Truth is, we may never really ever know the answer to that question. However, I believe we come here to learn, grow and love. When we are children, we are footloose and fancy-free. We are so curious about everything and look at the world through the eyes of wonder. We learn and develop our sense of sight, sound, smell, taste, and touch, discover our physical body, and learn how to interact with others. When we are young, we are quite connected to our multidimensional selves, including our connection to our soul and to the divine.

As we age, there are so many "rules and regulations" to live by that we fall in line as a young adult and learn about what we can or cannot do from our parents, siblings, teachers, friends, and work-life colleagues. We are defined by and buy into the expectations that others have placed on us. We go off figuring out the best way to learn what we should be doing to lead a good life, get ahead, and be successful. Our ego listens, learns, gets in line, and starts running the race towards where exactly? As our ego learns and grows, it gets stronger and louder. It wants to be in charge, control, judge, and whisper thoughts in our ears to keep us small and safe. We get on the hamster wheel, following the crowd, but here's the thing, all those "shoulds" drown out our very own soul. We forget that our soul has a plan, and it starts whispering into our ears about what's on our hearts in the quiet moments, about what we came here to do and to be. But are we listening? Do we hear our soul?

Our soul waits patiently until one day, there is such an earth-shattering event in our lives, and we are "broken open." We don't know what happened, and it's just an out-of-body experience. Our 3-dimensional shell is cracked open, some light gets into the cracks, and we begin to question everything we have ever learned to be true up until that point. We question everything. Our thoughts and beliefs, everything our parents or family taught us, what we were taught in school and society, and the rules we lived by in everyday life all get questioned. We wonder how our ego got in charge in the first place. Sadly, sometimes, this happens to us in childhood or even in our teen years, when it is even harder to navigate. If it hasn't happened to you yet, I believe it will happen. No soul on this planet will escape the struggles, the trials, the difficulties, or the lessons; Earth school is hard. I know firsthand, as I have had more than one of these events in my own life. When my first "broken open" moment occurred, a light bulb went off inside me, and I asked myself these 3 questions: 1) Who am I ? 2) Why am I here? 3) What's my purpose in this life?

When we have that "broken open moment," no matter how big or small, we often do what comes naturally to us; we try to protect ourselves and protect our own hearts, feelings, and emotions. We often turn away from the positive only to see the negative, feel the pain, and close down in anger and disappointment. However, we don't see that there is an equal amount of beauty, kindness, love, synchronicities, and magic available to us as well, but our heads are down, so focused on the space we are hiding in. Helen Keller once said, "When one door closes, another opens; but often we look so long at the closed door, that we do not see the one which has been opened for us." We are all sovereign beings, with free will to make our own choices in our lives. We individually have the power to decide which way to look, which path to take, what to believe, what to value, and what to hold sacred. Ultimately, we decide which perspective, and which set of colored glasses we should use to see the world we live in. What do you choose?

It takes faith and courage to move forward. I believe courage is defined as taking the first steps to your dream even if you can't see the path ahead. We can see the 3-dimensional world of beauty with our own eyes, including trees and mountains, oceans, rivers, lakes, flowers, birds, insects and all animals. We can see, feel, smell, and touch the beauty. We believe this is real because we can see, touch, and experience it. The tricky part is we can't see our soul. We may be able to feel it once we do the work to look within, deeper within ourselves, reaching for the deepest part of our being that we can access. Our soul will one day return to the oneness of creation and meld its energy with our creator. I was just listening to a conversation with Wayne Dwyer's (author and motivational speaker) daughters, Serena and Saje Dwyer, who said they had gotten messages from their dad, who passed in 2015. Wayne's soul says that he loves to meld his energy with the energy of the collective consciousness, and it is expansive and beautiful, but when he comes to give his daughters messages, he comes down as an individual energy. What does our soul take with us when our physical body dies? Our memories of who and what we have loved and what we have learned on planet Earth. Hopefully, if we are lucky, we will impart some of our wisdom and lessons to those we have loved along the way so that they can pass this wisdom and love onto the next person and create a ripple effect in this world. We leave everything else behind. Your life is a gift; choose wisely.

Have you answered Mary Oliver's question yet? ***"Tell me, what is it you plan to do with your one wild and precious life?"*** Let's face it: life is short, and we are only here for a short time. Steve Jobs, founder of Apple Inc., reminded us that "your time is limited, so don't waste it living someone else's life." Make your life count. Each struggle, trauma, or challenge that we experience is a lesson that makes us break open to let more light in and shine brighter, or it makes us shrink back, armor up against the next struggle, and dim our light. If you created a shell of safety in a bubble so as not to experience hurt or pain again and to be safe, let me ask you, "Is being safe living half a life?" Wouldn't you prefer to live a life of ALIVENESS filled with vibrancy, love and joy, happiness and adventure? The possibilities are endless to step into your power and create the life you choose. What do you choose? Do you say YES to yourself and your DREAM, or do you say NO and stay safe? Your soul knows what's on your heart; you just need to get quiet enough to listen to the whispers.

If you decide to say YES to yourself and step into the driver's seat of your own life, there are a few steps that you must take to THRIVE.

Step 1: BELIEVE in yourself and your dream.

If you have a DREAM, GOD put that in your heart for a reason. It's in YOUR heart, not your neighbors' or your friend's heart, but your heart. That passion, that talent, and stirring inside your heart is unique to you because only you hold the key to unlock that dream. Look inside yourself for your unique combinations of passions, gifts, skills, and talents. If you don't have a dream, it's time to dream again! What do you love? What are you good at? What makes time stand still for you when you do something? Is being creative, playing a sport, being analytical, problem solving or being a master musician one of your secret sauces? So much possibility and potential lives inside each of us. Believe that you are capable and have everything you need inside of you to realize your dream. You must BELIEVE in yourself with your whole heart and have the determination and perseverance to make it happen, no matter what.

Step 2: Create ENERGY & Take ACTION

Your dream should light that fire within and give you the energy to take the first step, and then taking action will continue the motivation and drive to keep going forward. Brendon Burchard (author, coach, and motivational speaker) explains the concept of energy in this way: "A power plant doesn't have energy, it generates energy." Just like a power plant, we must summon the energy within us each day with a positive mindset and belief system, as well as create physical energy in our body that will create a state of energy and positivity to get things done, to take action, and to accomplish our goals. We must generate our own energy, which must come from within us if we are to move the needle in our own life.

Taking the first step is the hardest; sometimes, taking those small steps requires a lot of energy. It probably takes the most energy to start. When something is stopped or immobile, it takes a great deal of energy to start moving it. Imagine how much energy a stopped train takes to get it moving, but once it's moving, the energy required to sustain its speed is much less. Let's look at the classic story" The Little Engine that Could" by Watty Piper. I remember reading it as a child, and what stuck with me was that no matter how small this little engine was, he created enough energy and was determined to move a larger stuck train up a large mountain for a good cause. The little blue engine was able to reach his goal through his positivity, open mind and willingness to try something new while chanting, "I think I can, I think I can I think I can" with pure determination and perseverance. Taking the first step is hard, but repetition helps our brain learn and wire faster. Steve Harvey says, "Jump" your parachute will open. You were meant for a big life, with miracles and magic! Don't Play Small.

Step 3: "Figure it Out" Attitude

Once you get in motion and start moving towards your goal, expect challenges and bumpy roads along the way. After all, it's life. What we can do is bring a positive attitude or an "I can figure it out" attitude to every situation. No matter what gets in your way of reaching your goal, know that you will face every challenge and will be able to figure it out. There are many ways to figure it out: you can learn how to do something yourself, take a class, find a mentor/advisor, or have someone do it for you. There is always a way. In this vast universe of potential and possibilities, you can always figure it out. Do Not Give Up. My grandmother, who left Ukraine when she was 20 years old during WW2, with my grandfather and my mom (who was 3 months old), left Ukraine for a dream of "A better life in the United States." She never looked back and never saw her parents or siblings again. Her motto was always "Keep Going," no matter what. Don't stop. Keep trying. Keep figuring it out. You will get there. Here's to you and your dream! I'm cheering you on!

Close

Thank you for taking this inner journey with me today from one person's perspective. I invite you to ponder the *"What ifs"* and take the time to sit with yourself in the quiet moments, start listening to your heart, disconnect from your ego, and let your soul lead the way. Your soul speaks through your heart and is that place of inner knowing without proof or explanation. I hope that you choose to (1) Rise - stand in your own powerful inner light, (2) Reconnect to your true authentic self and be guided by your heart and soul, and (3) Thrive by believing in yourself to go live the life you have imagined. I believe you were made for more!

***

Connect with Marie:

New podcast "Rise, Restore and Reconnect – Mind, Body and Spirit".

www.igniteyourbestself.com/podcast

Website: www.igniteyourbestself.com

Instagram: https://www.instagram.com/mariezunda_ignite/

LinkedIn: https://www.linkedin.com/in/marie-zunda-ma-cpcc-245ab839/

Melissa Williams-Gurian

Melissa Williams-Gurian is a highly sought-after executive coach, speaker, and organizational development consultant with over 25 years of experience helping CEOs and C-level executives navigate leadership challenges. As an expert in emotional intelligence, executive presence, and high-performance leadership, she has coached over 1,000 executives and leadership teams across Fortune 500 companies, mid-sized firms, and startups, in industries including technology, manufacturing, retail, finance, healthcare, entertainment, education, and nonprofits.

Melissa's philosophy is simple: knowing yourself is the foundation of leadership. *What do you believe? What do you want? What are you here to do?* When leaders recognize their own feelings, beliefs, and values, and how these principles drive their actions, they can have conversations that matter—the heart of great leadership. Melissa's methods help executives develop their self-awareness and emotional intelligence in order to build better relationships, communicate more effectively, and bring purpose and meaning to their work. Her work equips leaders with practical tools to create thriving, engaged teams.

Beyond coaching, Melissa is recognized as a thought leader, and speaks regularly on leadership, emotional intelligence and workplace culture. She is the author of two books, *How Do You Want To Show Up? Find Your Inner Truths—And Lead with Them*, and *How Do You Want To Show Up?* Workbook, and creates podcasts and articles for social media. She lives in Seattle with her husband, raising three children.

What Do Feelings Have to Do with Business? Everything!

by Melissa Williams-Gurian

Imagine being on a team phone call where tension is so thick you can feel it in your chest. A decision needs to be made, emotions are running high, and no one is on the same page. Or picture a difficult conversation with a colleague where you feel your breathing change and your shoulders tense as you sense conflict ahead.

What do these situations have in common? There are big feelings in play, and how they are handled will make a big difference to the outcome of each conversation.

Feelings are everywhere in the workplace

There's a misconception that emotions don't belong in the workplace. The truth is, feelings are everywhere at work, it's just that they usually go unacknowledged. They're a little like free radicals— highly reactive, unstable oxygen molecules. In the right conditions, they're helpful. In the wrong conditions, they're toxic.

Unless we pay attention to them, tune in to them, name and validate them, workplace feelings can wreak similar havoc. Not only do they cause stress to an individual, impacting how they show up in the workplace, but those emotions can also go free-roaming and make trouble with other people and teams. They can hinder productivity and create an unhappy, unmotivated company culture.

How Feelings Affect Your Work Life

Put yourself back into one of those emotionally charged moments I mentioned. How do you react? Do you notice and identify your emotions? Do you find a way to express yourself effectively and appropriately? Do you hide your negative emotions to keep the peace, or blast others with your anger or frustration? Do you consider what others might be feeling or experiencing, and try bringing some positive emotion to the conversation, to shift the dynamic?

The answers to these questions can make a big difference to your long-term success in your career and in your relationships with your family and friends. That's because our emotions can cause a ripple effect, changing how others show up, and helping to determine what is possible in any situation. It's not about choosing the perfect words or winning the argument. It's about being skilled with our emotions, and the emotions of others. This ability is also known as our emotional intelligence (referred to as EI or EQ): the ability to recognize and understand our own feelings, to recognize and understand the emotions of others, and to effectively bridge the space between the two.

In the chapter ahead, you'll learn about how your ability to manage and work with feelings can determine your success in life. You'll understand how that can change the responses of those around you, building better teams, businesses and organizations. Finally, you'll understand what it looks like to have relationships that honor feelings, and how to start creating them.

But first, I'll answer the question you may be asking yourself: what does any of this have to do with success?

Why Feelings Matter to Business and Your Own Success

A stereotype of a successful executive, popularized in fiction, is the image of an arrogant individualist who rises to the top alone. (They are always alone because no one can stand to be around them.) In fact, the truth about most successful leaders is far different.

Time and time again, research has shown that employees who have high emotional intelligence thrive in the workplace, out-earning and outperforming their peers.

For example, work by author, psychologist, and emotional intelligence expert Daniel Goleman indicates that, while innate smarts and technical skills might get you into a job, once you've met that threshold, what determines whether you move up the ladder is based almost entirely–90 percent!–on your ability to recognize and manage your own emotions, and recognize and influence others' emotions. Similarly, a study by business consultants TalentSmart found that leaders who function with high emotional intelligence outearn low-EQ professionals, often by a lot.

Why is this so? I've coached over 1,000 executives, in large corporations as well as start-ups, so I understand firsthand why this aspect of job performance means so much. People who don't identify and understand feelings get stuck in conversations that don't really matter. They argue, fail to listen, and alienate customers as well as colleagues. People who know how to identify and handle emotions, on the other hand, lead with strength and grace through changes, are better at spotting talent, and can give honest but empathetic feedback. Their understanding of feelings garners the admiration and trust of their employees. Unsurprisingly, those workers feel happier and more motivated, and are willing to go the extra mile for an emotionally connected leader.

Companies and organizations understand how important this is. So do business schools. For example, at Stanford University Graduate School of Business, the Interpersonal Dynamics class, known casually as the "Touchy Feely" class, has been the most popular elective for more than 45 years.

If you can improve your skill with emotions, you can boost productivity, engage your peers, and prevail in your field.

Who Am I? Recognizing Your Own Feelings

"Effective communication starts with the understanding that there is my point of view (my truth), and someone else's point of view (their truth)."

—From my book, How Do You Want to Show Up?

To start on this journey, you need to understand the one person you spend your entire life with: yourself. Getting clarity on your own feelings comes first.

Your presence, mindset, and emotional state influence the dynamics of a conversation, a meeting, or an entire team. Leadership isn't just about making decisions—it's about understanding the impact you have on others and how that affects collaboration, trust, and results.

In any given moment, you have a thought, a feeling, and a want. Together, those make up your inner compass, the lodestar you can use to guide you. Feelings are the hardest to identify of this triad. You might know your thoughts, you might have a sense of your wants, but do you know–with *precision*–how you feel at this very moment?

Here's how to find out.

Can you articulate how you feel and think at any given moment? If the answer is 'no,' you're not alone. Most people can only identify around three "feeling" words, typically "happy," "sad," and "angry". If that's you, consider starting a "feelings" notebook, which you can use to expand your feeling vocabulary and identify your emotions with specificity. In her bestselling book, *Atlas of the Heart*, author Brené Brown identified 87 different human emotions. Why are we restricting ourselves to three?

- Do you feel happy or overjoyed?
- Are you dissatisfied or heartbroken?
- Are you reserved or terrified?

This is so important in my work that I bring a "Feelings Chart" to meetings. It's a tool that lists dozens of different emotions to help my clients find the right word to describe how they are feeling. Naming their emotions helps them recognize their own point of view and why things matter to them, and also helps them articulate their position more clearly, allowing others to see who they are.

When we've identified our feelings, we can also track our emotions and look for patterns in how and when we have particular feelings. This work also helps us to process emotions, rather than pushing them aside. The better you are able to articulate how you feel, what you think, and what you believe, the more clarity you will have—and the more intentional you will become in stressful moments.

You won't simply react—you'll CHOOSE.

This isn't about expressing each feeling you have, but about recognizing those feelings, and then deciding on the impact you want to create. If you know you are feeling quiet, but you want to encourage your team, you can choose to put effort into projecting enthusiasm in the meeting, knowing that otherwise you might sound flat. If you're feeling nervous, you might practice breathing exercises before you go into a meeting, so that you can calm your fears and project confidence. Feelings can be contagious, so think about what kinds of emotions you'd like someone to "catch". Teams and even entire organizations or companies can become unproductive—even toxic—if negative emotions go unchecked.

Another way to cultivate emotional awareness is to think about which situations trigger your emotions.

- What makes you frustrated?
- What makes you feel overwhelmed?
- How do you typically respond when your buttons get pushed?

Knowing your triggers prepares you for those critical moments when fight or flight mode kicks in.

Your upbringing and life experiences play a major role in shaping your unconscious patterns and triggers, so reflecting on your history can give you a wealth of information.

- How did your family manage conflict?
- Was communication in your household direct or indirect?
- Were your parents strict or lenient?
- How did your birth order or role in the family shape expectations for you?

The present moment is also a great time to cultivate self-awareness. Pause at any time, and ask yourself:

"What am I feeling right now, and why?" Whether we're fearful, cheerful, delighted, or blue, how we feel in any given moment affects our energy, ability, and actions. If we can identify and pay attention to our emotions in the present moment, we can better take care of ourselves, and also act our best toward others.

Once you name the emotion, you can explore what triggered it. Was it what someone said? Was it the meaning you attached to their words? Your ability to recognize emotions in real time is what separates a reactive leader from an intentional one.

Seek Feedback to Understand Impact

You'll get even more information about yourself if you ask others how they experience you. I call this, "asking about your impact". You can try this at any time, but the most significant rewards come when you ask during a conversation, particularly one that might cause conflict.

Try these impact questions:

- What do you think about what I just said?
- How do you feel about what I just said?
- Is there anything else you are wanting from this conversation or from me?

Getting clear about our own emotions is the foundation of this work, but we need to build from there, to recognize how our actions, presence, and emotions shape the responses of those around us.

Who Are You? Understanding the Present Moment Feelings of Others

Understanding others doesn't come naturally to most of us—it requires effort and intention. We often jump to conclusions, assume we know someone's motivations, or listen just long enough to formulate our response.

Consider this startling fact: We live in the present moment, but our conversations tend to revolve around subjects related to the future or the past. We might discuss future goals, plans and strategies, or the past and what went right or wrong, and the lessons we learned (or didn't learn). We are less likely to talk about the present moment, including the actions, thoughts, and emotions of that moment.

If you want to differentiate yourself from others and improve your emotional intelligence, you can start by paying attention to what is happening for others in the present moment. Challenge yourself to observe, and to recognize which emotions are surfacing, who is engaged, and who might be withdrawing. From there, if you can, start a conversation about the emotions in the room. Naming them can change a conversation, moving it to one that matters, and can make a difference between a missed opportunity and a breakthrough moment for a team or group. Chances are, if you, or someone else, is feeling confused, frustrated, or bored, someone else is, too. Tuning in to your feelings provides valuable insights into the collective experience, helping guide the team forward.

Think of it this way: Be more interested than interesting.

- Instead of jumping to conclusions, get curious.
- Instead of assuming you know someone's motivations, ask.
- Instead of listening just to formulate a response, listen to understand.
- Instead of rushing to fix a problem, ask open-ended questions.

Consider asking:

- What do you think about what I just said?
- How do you feel about this decision?
- What's important to you in this situation?

Be aware that you also need to tune in during the answers. Being good at asking questions means listening actively. Instead of nodding along, ask follow-up questions so the person keeps sharing. For example, instead of responding to a frustrated colleague with, "I don't think that's true," try acknowledging their feelings, then following up with another question, "It sounds like this has been really challenging for you. Can you tell me more about what's been happening?"

Some other best practices for listening:

- Don't interrupt when others are talking.
- Listen to what's being said and what's not being said.
- Notice not only details of the conversation, but the larger picture.

I find that leaders are most present when they make a conscious decision just before an individual or team meeting to be all-in and engaged.

One more thought on understanding others' feelings: Some leaders worry that validating emotions is akin to agreeing with or even giving in to another person. This work is not about agreement, but about paying attention to feelings. Another way to say this is that it's about showing empathy, not sympathy. Sympathy is about feeling sorry for someone. Empathy is the ability to put ourselves in someone else's shoes, using our imagination to understand more about their perceptions, feelings, and point of view. We can then communicate back to a person that we have heard and acknowledged what they are expressing. Empathy helps people move forward and work together productively.

Now we'll explore the final question: Who are we? Because awareness of our feelings and the feelings of others is only part of the equation—fully realized emotional intelligence lies in what happens when we bring two or more people, perspectives, and truths together to create something bigger.

Who Are We: Creating a Culture of Emotional Intelligence

As I mentioned above, great leaders have the ability to pay attention to what's happening in the room in real time. To try this, take a moment to look at what's going on around you.

- What emotions are surfacing?
- Who is engaged? Who is shutting down?
- How is the team reacting to feedback?

As we've seen in the research, how you show up shapes the responses of those around you, and ultimately affects teams, businesses, and organizations–more than you think. Managing with emotional intelligence creates a feeling of psychological safety and motivation in which businesses and organizations thrive. How do you bring that to the team and the entire organization?

Create Norms

Emotionally skillful leaders make sure that people feel empowered to share feelings, needs and wants in the here and now. They are also prepared to take in what they hear in a way that lets everyone know it's safe to share positive AND negative feelings.

This can be as simple as:

- Establishing a norm of asking impact questions in meetings: "How do you feel about this decision?"
- Setting aside intentional team time, such as a meeting or retreat, to learn about each person as an individual.
- Encouraging leaders to acknowledge emotions in the room, for example, "I'm noticing that Susan has been quiet during this discussion. Susan, what are you feeling or thinking?"

Empathy is the Secret to Strong Relationships

Ban the phrase, "I'm sorry you feel that way". This commonly-used phrase is not an apology—it's a form of disengagement.

Try these alternatives:

- "It sounds like this really hurts."
- "You seem disappointed. Am I hearing that right?"
- "I heard you say you're frustrated. You'd like to move on and talk about sales. Is that right?"

Without acknowledgement of feelings, conversations become battles where each person fights to be heard. No one changes their views unless they feel understood.

Instead of:

"You're overreacting."

Try:

"It sounds like something is important here. Can you tell me more about what's been happening?"

Instead of: " I don't think you should feel that way"

Try: " I can see how you might feel isolated. Tell me more about that. I really want to understand your experience."

When people feel seen and heard, they become more open to understanding you in return. A leader who validates others' experiences, honors different perspectives, and acknowledges emotions becomes an irreplaceable asset to any team or organization.

Integrating Emotional Intelligence Into Your Life

Who am I? Who are you? Who are we together?

Now that you understand these three questions, you may feel daunted by the work ahead. But emotional intelligence is a skill—one that can be learned, practiced, and strengthened over time.

Getting better at it starts with setting your own intentions. The sooner you get started, the sooner you'll see these changes.

Commit to a few small actions, then build from there:
- Have a difficult conversation.
- Practice self-reflection.
- Validate someone else's experience.

True collaboration happens when we integrate both of our experiences—when my reality and yours are acknowledged, understood, and respected. Strong relationships generate trust, creativity, and momentum, enabling them to move beyond individual perspectives and build something greater together. In my over 25 years of experience helping CEOs, senior executives, and leadership teams navigate complex business challenges, I've watched as leaders learned to acknowledge, name and validate feelings, then took these skills to their meetings and experienced the delight of building lasting bridges with others. At the end of those meetings, they walked away knowing about the internal experiences of others, having experienced their colleagues in a full, vulnerable way. This work brings humanity to the workplace, and the connection and communication leads to better results, every time, with fewer "free radicals" getting in the way. END

***

Contact Information:

To contact Melissa, buy her book, and learn more about her work, visit: www.melissawilliamsgurian.com

Instagram: @melissagurianw

LinkedIn: www.linkedin.com/in/melissa-williams-gurian

Find her books on Amazon.com, available in paperback or Kindle

Author photo © 2025 Ingrid Pape-Sheldon Photography

Robert Ndoping

Robert Ndoping is a Performance Consultant, Executive Strategy Coach, Trainer, and Client Success Strategist with a proven track record in leadership development, business coaching, and client success management. He specializes in helping executives, teams, and organizations enhance strategic execution, optimize performance, and drive sustainable growth.

As CEO of Ndoping & Co. Performance Consultants, Robert has designed and facilitated 100+ leadership and strategy workshops, empowering organizations to improve team cohesion, increase productivity by 40%, and enhance sales performance by 25%. His data-driven coaching approach helps businesses navigate challenges and unlock peak performance.

As National Client Success Manager at Windmill Microlending, he has elevated client engagement, increased satisfaction by 25%, and maintained a 94% Net Promoter Score. His coaching, process optimization, and operational leadership expertise ensure long-term client success and retention.

Robert has lived experiences across seven countries and three continents. He holds a BSc in the Science of Politics, dual Master's degrees in Welfare Policies and International Development from Lund University, Sweden, and an MBA certificate in Strategy and Performance from the Rotman School of Management—University of Toronto, Canada. He is also an Associate Certified Business Coach from the International Coaching Federation.

Driven by a passion for strategic leadership and transformation, Robert helps leaders and businesses achieve clarity, efficiency, and measurable success.

Resilience: A Journey to Find Purpose

By Robert Ndoping

A stone tossed into a rushing river does not remain the same. The current drags it, tumbles it, and grinds it against the riverbed. What was once jagged and rough becomes smooth and refined—a thing of beauty admired by many. While it could have shattered and been reduced to sand, it endured the harsh current of the transformation process, which is resilience.

My life has been shaped by resilience, having come through the harsh current of life's experiences and circumstances. I was born in Cameroon – a country shaped by colonial history and once a protectorate of both France and Britain. A land rich in culture and diversity, known as "Africa in miniature," with over 250 ethnic groups. Yet, like many former colonies, Cameroon remains burdened by corruption, political instability, and limited opportunities. Opportunities are so limited that they rob you of the ability to dream of a future. Despite these limitations, I knew one thing: I was born with an innate desire to help others. I knew this even when I did not know much about assisting myself. In the words of Muhammad Ali, "Service to others is the rent you pay for your room here on earth." It wasn't clear how or in what capacity, but I was drawn to supporting others and being a part of something greater than myself. My family was middle-class, with both parents working as civil servants, which typically means we got by. But I couldn't ignore the poverty surrounding me, riddled with young people my age who appeared to be lost or in need. I wanted to find a solution. I wanted to be a solution. So began my strive for a solution with the typical middle-class ambition of working for the government. I could change the system if I worked for the government, and convincingly so. I pursued a Political Science and Public Administration degree, completed my training at the local government institute, and secured a position in the Cameroonian government. My parents couldn't be prouder!

I was the youngest staff member in my provincial department, eager and trying to prove myself. Then, an opportunity opened that would change the course of my career. My new boss, a high-ranking finance official, walked into my office one day and handed me a file. "Robert, you will be presenting at the annual provincial meeting next month," she said. "I'll be there to listen to you. And I know you can do this. "Fear surged through me – the kind that runs through your spine. How could someone with the least experience in the department be chosen to speak in front of the governor and provincial ministers? What if I failed? What if I embarrassed myself? But my boss believed in me. Then I remembered Henry Ford's words: "Whether you think you can or can't, you're right." That belief became my fuel. I prepared rigorously, practicing in front of the mirror and refining my speech. On the day of the meeting, dressed in my best suit, I stood before the audience and delivered my presentation. When I finished, the room erupted in applause. That moment was a turning point, igniting my confidence and cementing my path forward. Remember that "every time you make the hard, correct decision, you become a bit more courageous, and every time you make the easy, wrong decision, you become a bit more cowardly" (Ben Horowitz). My performance at that meeting did not go unnoticed. Soon after, I became a sought-after speaker within my province, delivering presentations at various governmental and community events. My name gained recognition among influential people, and I found myself in rooms I once only dreamed of entering. My growing reputation and demonstrated leadership eventually led to a well-deserved promotion within the government, allowing me more responsibilities and the ability to influence policies in ways I had always aspired to. My passion for development grew beyond the borders of my country. I wanted to contribute not just to Cameroon but to the world. That pursuit led me to Sweden in 2007, where I enrolled in an MSc in Development Studies. It was a fresh start, a new continent, a new way of life, and a new set of challenges.

The shift was overwhelming at first. The cultural differences were stark, replacing the warmth of familiar culture and traditions that once surrounded me. I found myself in a society that valued independence and individualism in ways I had never experienced. The food differed –Swedish cuisine emphasized dairy, seafood, and open-faced sandwiches. This was worlds apart from the leafy, colourful, - and flavorful dishes of Cameroon. The language barrier was another hurdle. Although many Swedes spoke English, navigating daily life without fluency in Swedish made simple tasks, like reading signs or grocery shopping, quite challenging. Moreover, the approach to work and education was strikingly different. Where hierarchy was deeply embedded in the professional landscape of Cameroon, Sweden thrived on egalitarianism, where students and young people in general were encouraged to challenge authority and voice their opinions freely. Adjusting to this new lifestyle took quite a toll on my young self, especially having left the security of a career and the familiarity of home for the uncertainty of a foreign land. The cold Scandinavian winters were unforgiving, and financial constraints forced me to take on transitional jobs. There were nights when I questioned my decision and times when I wanted to give up. But I held on.

Two years passed, and I graduated. But I wasn't done. I pursued another MSc in International Welfare Policies, expanding my expertise. My studies took me across Europe, broadening my understanding of global development. Living and studying in different countries exposed me to various lifestyles, social systems, and professional cultures. The UK's fast-paced environment and structured academic setting encouraged critical thinking and innovation. In contrast, Denmark's emphasis on work-life balance and collaborative learning introduced me to new problem-solving approaches. These experiences expanded my academic knowledge and taught me adaptability and resilience in navigating diverse cultural and professional landscapes. The exposure to multiple governance models, economic strategies, and social policies deepened my insight into global development. This exposure solidified my desire to contribute meaningfully to policy-making and international aid efforts. I worked tirelessly, enduring exhaustion to chase a dream beyond my reach. "Success is not final; Failure is not fatal. It is the courage to continue that count" (Winston Churchill).

Denmark became the next chapter of my journey. I moved as a Green Card holder, starting from scratch again. I worked transitional jobs before securing a volunteer position at the Danish Refugee Council, where I supported displaced communities in over 40 countries. That role soon became a full-time position, and eventually, I became a manager. My time at the Danish Refugee Council was transformative in many ways. I gained firsthand insight into the complexities of humanitarian work, understanding the delicate balance between immediate relief efforts and long-term sustainability. Working with displaced populations exposed me to resilience in its rawest form – families rebuilding their lives from nothing, children finding joy in minor victories, and communities striving to regain a sense of normalcy amid the turmoil. Real change requires patience, cultural sensitivity, and an unwavering commitment to ethical leadership. Managing teams across different projects also sharpened my ability to navigate cross-cultural collaborations, build stakeholder trust, and implement impactful programs in challenging environments. These lessons would later shape my approach to leadership and strategy in international development and beyond. I had achieved what I once envisioned – working in international development settings and impacting global poverty alleviation. Yet, I couldn't shake off the feeling of wanting more.

My friends in Canada encouraged me to consider moving to North America. They believed my skills were better suited for the opportunities there. Hesitatingly, I went on a first visit. What ultimately convinced me was the appeal of the Canadian economy – its openness to skilled immigrants, the stability of its job market, and the abundant opportunities for professional growth. Canada's strong support for diversity and inclusion meant that my international development and leadership background could be valued and utilized. The country's structured immigration system also provided a clear pathway to permanent residency and career advancement, which was an attractive prospect after navigating uncertain job markets in Europe. Seeing the vast potential for making a difference professionally and personally, I knew it was time to embrace the next chapter of my journey. I left Denmark for Canada, arriving in Calgary in mid-February – welcomed by a winter I had never experienced. Welcomed by the blistering cold, I questioned my decision every other day. Had I made the right choice? Will it be worth it? As I struggled with answering my questions, somewhere in there, I was reminded that growth requires a bit of discomfort.

In Canada, I started again. I am tempted to say I started again from scratch, going by the insistence of "Canadian work experience" by employers, making it challenging to find employment despite all my international work experience. I persevered and took up volunteering, networking, and eventually securing roles aligned with my passion and long-term goals. I worked with organizations supporting immigrants, helping skilled professionals navigate the complexities of establishing careers in a new country. I was inching closer to feeling complete as I worked in the development sector and rose into leadership positions. Amongst my jobs in Canada, Windmill Microlending played a pivotal role in helping me reflect on my purpose. As the Client Success program manager, I led a team of success coaches across Canada, empowering skilled immigrants to overcome barriers and achieve their professional aspirations. This role brought me to ask myself: what is my true purpose? What is that one thing I am meant to do?

After a series of profound reflections, I found the common thread in everything I had done. Through supporting, building, guiding, and mentoring lay the very essence of coaching. I realized that I had been a coach without the title. It was time to formalize that calling. I pursued certification through the International Coaching Federation, completed an MBA certification course in strategy and performance optimization, and earned additional qualifications. Ndoping & Co. Strategy Coaching was born and continues to thrive as a firm dedicated to empowering businesses, leaders, and professionals to navigate challenges with strategy to achieve breakthroughs.

Coaching is more than a profession to me. It is a transformative journey that empowers individuals to craft a clear plan to drive personal transformation, set clear goals, and take meaningful action, enough to give me a reason to wake up the next day. I finally found my purpose, but, in a way, my purpose finally found me. Coaching found me! Throughout my career, I had unknowingly applied the principles of coaching by listening actively, asking the right questions, and guiding people toward solutions that best suited their needs. Coaching gave me a framework to harness these skills and amplify my impact. It taught me the power of accountability, the importance of mindset shifts, and the role of structured guidance in personal and professional growth. Coaching not only strengthened my ability to support others but also gave me clarity on my aspirations. It reinforced that authentic leadership is not about having all the answers but empowering others to find their paths. As I embarked on this new career phase, I realized that coaching was not just a job but a calling that aligned perfectly with my lifelong purpose of building, guiding, and supporting others. I realized that I had been a coach without the title. It was thrilling when I formalized it. It was deeply fulfilling to live my purpose as a coach finally.

Resilience carried me through each chapter of my life. That ability to adapt, endure, and push forward despite life's storms. Resilience is about surviving hardship and thriving in the face of adversity. It is about learning from setbacks, using failure as a foundation for growth, and embracing uncertainty with unwavering determination. With each challenge I encountered, from leaving my home country to starting over in new environments, my ability to remain steadfast was tested. Resilience taught me that discomfort is often the precursor for transformation. Every closed door, every obstacle, and every harrowing moment shaped my ability to strategize, innovate, and persevere. More importantly, resilience reinforced the understanding that success is not a straight path but a series of challenges that must be navigated with courage and determination. By developing resilience, I have turned difficulties into stepping stones, proving repeatedly that perseverance and adaptability can overcome even the most daunting circumstances. This recalls Gregory Williams' words: "On the other side of a storm is the strength that comes from having navigated through it. Raise your sail and begin." I have faced rejection with doors shut right in my face. I have experienced setbacks that make you question your life as it is. In all, I refused to be defined by these and chose to turn them into steppingstones.

I share my journey as a story of personal success, a work in progress, and an invitation for you to reflect on yours. What is your purpose? Take some time to chew on this question. What is your purpose? While chewing on it, I'd like to remind you that one's purpose is beyond personal achievement. It is about impact and how your journey influences those around you. True fulfillment comes when we align our strengths, passions, and experiences to serve the greater good. Have you considered the legacy you want to leave behind?

What difference can you make in someone's life? The world is shaped by those who dare to believe in their potential and step forward with conviction. As you step forward with conviction, remember that life is not meant to be lived passively. "I've learned that mistakes can often be as good a teacher as success." (Jack Welch). In our struggles, we discover strength in our challenges; we uncover wisdom. Through the passive, non-linear and challenging currents of life, let resilience power you through. Thankfully, you are not alone; I have been where you are and will be here for you. "Life is fragile. We're not guaranteed a tomorrow, so give it everything you've got." (Tim Cook). Reach out to me as your accountability partner, and let's tap into your strengths, which are powered by resilience, together. You are not alone!

***

Contact information:

Email: coaching@ndopingco.com

Website: www.ndopingco.com

Phone: *403-617-0191*

Facebook: *Ndoping Coaching*

Instagram: *Ndoping_co*

YouTube: www.youtube.com/@ndopingcoaching4183

Cynthia Laden Newman

Sustainable Growth Creator | Financial Services Executive Coach

Cynthia Laden Newman is a Financial Services Executive Coach and the founder of Success Strategists and The Seeds of Change Foundation. Through Success Strategists, she helps professionals to unlock their potential, transform challenges into opportunities, and achieve sustainable success. Through Seeds of Change, she is dedicated to empowering underserved communities by expanding access to educational opportunities, and social impact initiatives.

With over 40 years of experience in the financial services industry, Cynthia's career is defined by strategic vision, leadership development, and driving sustainable growth. A former Managing Director at Morgan Stanley, she advanced from Client Service Associate to Financial Advisor, Sales Manager, Training Manager, Branch Manager, Complex Manager, and Regional Director, demonstrating an exceptional ability to cultivate leadership, expand market presence, and foster high-performing teams.

Cynthia specializes in coaching executives, advisors, and teams in business strategy, leadership excellence, time management, and client engagement. Her results-driven approach fosters high-performance cultures, helping professionals implement systems for success while delivering first-class client service.

A recognized industry expert, Cynthia delivers impactful coaching, workshops, and keynotes, blending personal development with professional growth. Through Success Strategists, she shares her wealth of experience with both emerging and established leaders, guiding them through obstacles and positioning them for long-term success.

Cynthia's work has influenced countless professionals across the financial services industry. She is passionate about fostering resilience, shaping innovation, and creating lasting impact. She welcomes opportunities to collaborate with organizations and individuals seeking transformational growth.

Looking Back:
A Life Shaped by Challenges and Opportunities

By Cynthia Laden Newman

My life has been a journey of unexpected challenges, transformative opportunities, and defining experiences. I was raised in New Jersey, where my early years were filled with comfort and familiarity. However, at the age of nine, my world expanded dramatically when my family moved to New York City. The city's energy opened my eyes to possibilities beyond what I had known.

At sixteen, I embarked on a life-changing journey through South America and Europe, culminating in a transatlantic voyage. Visiting remote Andean and Amazonian villages challenged my perception of abundance. The contrast between my life and theirs was striking. I had grown up with every modern convenience, yet these communities thrived in ways that extended beyond material wealth. Despite limited resources, they cultivated joy, strength, and deep bonds. At that moment, I realized that true happiness and fulfillment did not come from material possessions but from relationships, the sense of purpose they provide, and the communities they create. More importantly, this realization sparked a deeper question: How could I use my resources to make a meaningful impact in the world?

Upon returning to the United States, I continued my education at the University of Oregon and later graduated from the University of Vermont. College presented academic challenges that tested my determination, but overcoming them reinforced the value of perseverance and hard work, both of which proved invaluable throughout my career.

Breaking Barriers in Finance

My career in finance began at Merrill Lynch in 1982. I started as a sales assistant and quickly obtained my licenses and registrations. Observing financial advisors at work, I realized I could do this job and do it well. However, as a young woman of 22 in a male-dominated industry, I faced significant challenges. I had no established network or influential connections. Despite these setbacks, I refused to let them hinder my professional growth.

Determined to find a training program, I pursued every opportunity until a manager at Drexel Burnham took a chance on me. Their rigorous program placed me among highly driven professionals who helped sharpen my sales skills. Those early years were defined by discipline, tenacity, and growth. I spent long nights studying market trends and perfecting sales presentations, knowing that each step brought me closer to achieving my goal of financial independence.

By the mid-1980s, I had built momentum in my career, expanding my business at Drexel Burnham's Beverly Hills office. After marrying my husband, we relocated to Los Angeles, where I worked with high-net-worth clients. This experience strengthened my expertise and confidence. However, when Drexel Burnham collapsed in 1989, I had to reassess my firm choices. After extensive due diligence, I transitioned my business to Merrill Lynch, where I adapted to a more bureaucratic environment. The transition challenged my resilience and reaffirmed the necessity of staying true to my core values.

Five years later, I transitioned my business to PaineWebber, which later became UBS. This move returned me to an entrepreneurial environment where I thrived. My business flourished during this time, and my husband joined my team, marking the beginning of my shift towards management.

At UBS, I advanced into leadership roles as Sales Manager, Training Manager, and Associate Branch Manager. After ten years, it became clear that opportunities for women in management were limited. In 2004, seeking greater professional growth, I joined Morgan Stanley as the Downtown Los Angeles Branch Manager. This move expanded my leadership abilities in ways I had not imagined.

My sixteen years at Morgan Stanley were filled with both milestones and setbacks. During my first five years, I worked under exceptional leaders who supported my growth and recognized my achievements. One of the most defining moments in my career came when I was promoted to Complex Manager in Beverly Hills. This pivotal moment could have been even more impactful with the guidance of an executive coach. Leading this large operation required me to manage my relationship with senior leadership, support and develop my team, and balance the diverse needs of employees at every level.

When Morgan Stanley acquired Smith Barney in 2009, leadership changed, and firm politics intensified. I had to reapply for my role, clearly articulate my value, and demonstrate my leadership impact. This process sharpened my ability to advocate for myself. I secured my role and continued advancing in my career. As a result of my efforts, I was promoted to Regional Director, stepping into a new level of leadership with its own unique challenges.

After just fifteen months, a reorganization eliminated several Regional Director positions, including mine. I was reassigned to the Pasadena, California Complex, a struggling market. Although the two firms had officially consolidated three years earlier, this market operated as if they were still two separate entities. Despite these obstacles, I focused on strengthening my team, driving business growth, and optimizing operational efficiency. As a result, we accomplished our goals, and the Pasadena Complex consistently ranked among the top five complexes in the country.

Reflecting on my career, I recognize that I repeatedly broke barriers in an industry not always welcoming to women. Time and again, I was the only woman in the room. I worked twice as hard to earn respect relying on perseverance and excellence.

In hindsight, an executive coach could have provided the insight and mentorship needed to navigate pivotal moments more effectively. Leadership requires anticipating challenges, managing office dynamics, and maintaining clarity under pressure. The right coach could have helped me identify blind spots, refine my leadership approach, and make strategic decisions.

Successful CEOs and elite athletes rely on multiple coaches to help them reach their highest potential. While I broke barriers on my own, I now understand the power of a strong support system in sustaining long-term success. No one achieves greatness alone, and the right coach could have made all the difference in my journey.

Resilience and Leadership

Resilience and leadership are not just learned; they are forged through adversity. Throughout my career, I have faced moments that tested my strength and challenged my confidence. Each experience shaped my ability to navigate setbacks, advocate for myself, and empower those around me.

Building trust and credibility in a competitive industry requires preparation, determination, and execution. One of my most vivid memories from my time at Drexel Burnham was meeting with an ultra-high-net-worth prospect who doubted my abilities. I conducted thorough preparation and created a customized investment plan. By the end of the conversation, the prospect decided to become a client. That experience reinforced a powerful lesson: preparation, determination, and execution can dismantle even the toughest barriers.

I soon realized that these same qualities of preparation, confidence and resilience were just as important when I faced one of my first confrontations as a Financial Advisor and young mother at Merrill Lynch. After having my first child, I requested a transfer to a different office, believing it would allow me to better balance my career and family life. I was told I could move, but my book of business would have to remain behind. The only way to retain what I had rightfully built was to threaten legal action. That experience reinforced the importance of standing up for myself and advocating for what I had earned through hard work.

Another significant challenge came when I worked under a Regional Director whose leadership style was demeaning and dismissive. He repeatedly humiliated me in public, creating a toxic work environment. Rather than discouraging me, his patronizing attitude strengthened my resolve, reinforcing my decision to resign and pursue better opportunities. Reflecting on that experience, I recognize that it taught me an invaluable lesson in self-worth and the importance of prioritizing environments where my skills and contributions would be valued.

This experience also deepened my understanding of trust in leadership, a lesson that would be tested in my career. At one point, a team member I mentored and supported deliberately attempted to have me removed from my role. That experience forced me to reassess whom I trusted and the people I chose to surround myself with. It was a difficult but necessary lesson that reinforced the importance of being highly selective in whom I trusted and the people I chose to surround myself with.

Perseverance has always been the foundation of my success. There were times when everything seemed to be falling apart. Business deals collapsed, economic downturns created uncertainty, and internal politics threatened my advancement. In those moments, I reminded myself that every setback is an opportunity to learn, grow, and refine my leadership style.

Leadership is about creating an environment where others can thrive. I prioritized making sure my teams felt valued, appreciated, and supported, knowing that collective success is always greater than individual achievement. Over time, I realized that leadership is not just about treating people with dignity and respect but also about recognizing their unique strengths and adapting to their needs. The ability to analyze and respond to differences was essential for creating a productive and engaging work environment.

One of the greatest joys of leadership has been mentoring young professionals. I have always found fulfillment in identifying and nurturing talent, whether by helping someone overcome self-doubt or guiding them through firm dynamics. Leadership has never been about personal accolades. It has always been about creating a legacy of empowered individuals who continue to drive success long after I have moved on. Great leadership is rooted in the ability to listen. Some of the most profound moments in my career came from engaging in meaningful conversations and genuinely hearing the concerns of my colleagues. My goal was never to provide immediate solutions but to acknowledge their experiences and collaborate to find the best way forward.

Successful leadership is not about having all the answers but about asking the right questions. I encouraged my teams to think critically, challenge the status quo, and bring innovative ideas to the table. My goal was to help them recognize their independence, value their contributions, and understand their role in shaping the organization's success.

As I progressed in my leadership journey, I came to understand that leadership is about service rather than authority. My role was to remove obstacles, provide the necessary tools for success, and empower my team. When supporting others became my primary focus, I witnessed incredible growth. People felt valued, engaged, and motivated to work toward a shared vision.

The lessons in perseverance and leadership have shaped my business philosophy, influenced my coaching practice, and transformed my approach to personal and professional growth. Leadership is not a destination but a continuous journey of learning and adapting.

The Shift to Coaching

Leaving corporate leadership was one of the most difficult transitions of my life. My identity had been so deeply tied to my role as a Managing Director at Morgan Stanley that stepping away felt like losing a part of myself. During that time, my family's support and reassurance were invaluable. They encouraged me to pause, reflect, and rediscover my purpose.

As I took time to reflect, several people reached out for guidance on career and business development. That was when I realized that coaching was the natural next step. Helping others succeed had always been the most rewarding aspect of my leadership roles. Becoming an executive coach felt like the next evolution of my career, as if every experience up to that point had prepared me for this moment.

Through this process, I came to understand that my many years as a corporate leader had never been just about metrics and profitability. They had been about people, their aspirations, and struggles, and the guidance they needed to achieve their goals. This shift in perspective reignited my passion and gave me a renewed sense of purpose for the next phase of my career.

As I built my coaching practice, I recognized familiar challenges. Many of these professionals faced the same struggles I had once encountered. Business development, self-doubt, office politics, and career stagnation often held them back. I saw an opportunity to provide real-world solutions, meaningful guidance, and a clear path to success. Every successful CEO or professional athlete has a coach to help them navigate challenges. I wanted to provide that same level of support to my clients.

Now, as an executive coach, I help professionals overcome the very challenges I once faced. I provide the guidance I wish I had, offering insights gained through real-world experiences. My clients range from financial advisors striving for business growth to teams navigating complex dynamics to leaders optimizing their business strategies. The common thread among them is a desire to elevate their performance and understand that the right support can be pivotal for professional development.

For me, coaching is not just about giving advice. It is about active listening, understanding each client's unique challenges, and empowering them to co-create solutions. My years of leadership have equipped me with the ability to ask the right questions, help clients shift their perspectives, and inspire meaningful action. I also draw upon lessons from my own life, including resilience, adaptability, and the importance of taking calculated risks to guide my clients through their journeys. My experiences are invaluable to them.

Building my coaching practice required commitment, continuous learning, and a willingness to evolve. I pursued additional certifications, attended industry conferences, and built a strong network of professionals who referred clients to me. I quickly learned that credibility was essential. People wanted to work with someone who had successfully navigated similar challenges.

As my client base grew, I felt tremendous fulfillment in seeing the tangible results of my work. Each success story, every shift in a client's mindset, and every breakthrough they achieved reinforced my passion for coaching. It became more than just a career; it became my purpose. Today, I am dedicated to expanding my business, developing new programs, and mentoring the next generation of leaders.

If there is one lesson I have learned, it is that reinvention is possible at any stage of life. No matter the setbacks or challenges, there is always an opportunity to pivot, grow, and create a new path forward.

Key Take Aways from Building my Executive Coaching Business

Listen Deeply

Effective coaching begins with truly hearing your clients. It is not just about listening to their words but also about understanding the emotions and challenges beneath them. Listening is an art, and mastering it has been crucial in building trust and rapport. Deep listening involves asking the right questions, using gentle probing, and helping clients explore the root of their challenges.

Build Trust

Trust is the foundation of any coach-client relationship. My first consultation always focuses on making clients feel heard and understood in a supportive environment. I have found that trust is not built overnight but is earned through consistent action and genuine care. It requires honesty, clarity, and reliability.

Empower the Client

My role is not to provide direct answers but to guide clients toward discovering their own. This process builds autonomy and confidence. By challenging clients to think independently for themselves and take ownership of their decisions, I help them develop resilience and self-assurance.

The Importance of Consistency

Clients who commit to regular coaching sessions see the most success. Growth does not happen through quick fixes but through long-term effort and self-development. Regular discussions, reviews, and assessments keep progress on track and maintain momentum. Consistency builds accountability, helping clients stay committed to their goals.

Invest in Yourself

Investing in yourself is essential for long-term success. Whether it is hiring an executive coach, enhancing your skills, or prioritizing personal growth, these investments pay off. Many professionals hesitate to invest in themselves, but those who do often experience greater career satisfaction and advancement.

Adaptability

The business world is constantly evolving, and staying open to change has been a key factor in my success. Adaptability is not only about navigating change but also means understanding the unique needs of each client. The ability to tailor my approach to their specific circumstances has been instrumental in their growth and success.

Clarity of Vision

Having a clear vision means developing a well-defined understanding of your long-term goals, values and aspirations. It serves as a roadmap, ensuring that every action you take aligns with your future. Setting long-term goals and breaking them into actionable steps helps creates a roadmap for success.

Celebrate Success

Acknowledging and celebrating progress, no matter how small, is a powerful motivator. Recognizing achievements reinforces the value of hard work and dedication. Reflecting on milestones, whether achieving a breakthrough or receiving positive feedback, creates momentum and inspires continuous growth.

Entrepreneurship is more than just strategy and goals; it is about staying true to oneself, building meaningful relationships and committing to lifelong learning. These lessons have profoundly shaped my coaching practice while also contributing to my growth. They have reinforced the power of resilience, confidence and the belief that success is always within reach.

Making a Difference in Society and Leaving a Lasting Legacy

Beyond my family and success in business, the most meaningful part of my journey has been the impact I have made through giving back. In 2013, my husband and I adopted Nelson, a teenager from the Home of Hope Orphanage in Malawi, Africa. This decision profoundly changed our family's lives. The adoption process was a transformative experience that taught me invaluable lessons about empathy and the importance of creating opportunities for those in need.

Our commitment to giving back did not stop with adoption. We established a foundation dedicated to supporting a variety of initiatives. One of our first major projects was funding a soccer field at the orphanage. More than just a place to play, it became a source of joy, companionship, and a sense of normalcy for the children who live there.

Our efforts expanded beyond this initial project. We have awarded scholarships, improved schools, and provided essential resources. Every contribution, no matter how small, brings us one step closer to creating lasting change.

Remaining actively involved is a priority for our board. We stay in close contact with various organizations to assess the impact of our initiatives and ensure they are making a difference. These experiences continue to remind me that true success is not just about personal achievement; it is about using our success to uplift others and create opportunities for those who need them most.

Building this foundation became a collaborative effort that strengthened our relationships with family and friends while deepening our shared sense of purpose. Witnessing the tangible impact we are making has been one of life's greatest joys. I have come to realize that true success is not solely measured by professional achievements but by the positive legacy we leave behind and the lives we touch along the way.

A Call to Action

The message I want to share with readers is simple: believe in yourself. No matter how difficult a situation may seem, trust that you have the ability to overcome it. Success begins with a clear vision, a willingness to take action, and the determination to keep moving forward. Create a plan, seize opportunities, and stay focused on growth. When you achieve success, pay it forward. True success is not just about personal accomplishment but also about lifting others along the way.

***

If you are ready to take that step, I would love to connect.

Website at successtrategists.com

LinkedIn at linkedin.com/in/Cynthia-laden-newman

Email at cynthia@successtrategists.com.

Let's work together to unlock your full potential and create a future of limitless possibilities.

Amber McMillan

Amber McMillan is a transformational leader, executive educator, and impact coach with over 30 years of experience in nonprofit and for profit governance, interest holder engagement, and leadership development. As a Certified Volunteer Administrator (CVA) and former Board Chair of the International Council for Certification in Volunteer Administration, she has spent decades guiding individuals and organizations toward purposeful leadership, fostering equity and driving systemic change.

Passionate about the intersection of self-worth and leadership, Amber has worked with municipal and Indigenous governments, global organizations, and thousands of professionals, helping them navigate the evolving landscape of work with clarity and confidence. As Region Mentor for the Pacific Northwest of the Americas with the Project Management Institute (PMI), she empowers leaders to embrace change, redefine success, and lead from a place of authenticity.

Her journey—shaped by years of striving, self-discovery, and a radical redefinition of worth—led her to contribute to this powerful book. In her chapter she challenges conventional wisdom around productivity and success, offering a new framework for fulfillment in both work and life.

When she's not writing or coaching, Amber can be found paddling in the Pacific Ocean in either a dragon boat or outrigger canoe, mentoring future leaders as a university professor teaching project and change management, and championing the power of self-awareness as a catalyst for cracking the rich code.

Worth Ethic:
Redefining Work Ethic Through the Lens of Self-Worth

By Amber McMillan

I think you and I have been lied to.

I think we have maintained that success is built on how hard we work and what we accomplish; the more we sacrifice and grind, the more success we achieve. But no matter how hard the work is, the end goal seems to keep moving. And, it leaves many of us feeling burnt out, questioning our purpose and no closer to 'cracking the rich code' of fulfillment.

What if the lie is that we've been chasing the wrong goal? What if the key to success isn't about how much we do, but about how much we value who we are?

For years I prided myself on how many projects I could work on. I was the first-to-arrive and last-to-leave person and I worked through discomfort, hid my infirmities, and often survived on little sleep to prove my dedication. I said 'yes' more than 'no' and chased opportunities like my worth depended on it. This hustle became my modern religion where worshipping busyness was my ultimate virtue.

But, I became weary and unfulfilled. I pondered those who effortlessly pursued their passions, declining opportunities that didn't align with their goals. I questioned if true accomplishment wasn't solely about effort, but also about recognizing my inherent value and letting it guide my actions.

What if my childhood experiences, societal pressures, and cultural expectations had gifted me a distorted view of my worth—and by reframing that perspective, I could unlock fulfillment and authentic success?

The Seeds of Worth

When I look to my own childhood, I see it littered with praise over my accomplishments. Raised by entrepreneurial parents, I spent much of my time immersed in business conversations, late night meetings, and the relentless marathon of work ethic. I recognize today that my parents were not just motivated by working hard, but by proving they deserved the opportunity to work *harder*. The message I received was that effort equaled value, and that the work was never truly done.

As a child, I didn't question this rhythm as it was simply the air I breathed. Watching my parents chase new opportunities, navigate challenges, and push past their limits taught me a great deal about perseverance and resilience. What I was not self-aware of was how it also planted a deep belief in my mind that my worthiness was tied to how much I could achieve. Even as I excelled at things, there was always the next goal to hit, task to conquer, and the quiet fear that doing less might make me less.

It wasn't until decades later that I began to recognize this pattern in my life. I started to realize how often I'd put myself in situations like this, chasing validation from others who were either unwilling or unable to give it to me. Whether it was teachers, mentors or even friends, I found myself working overtime to prove that I was worthy, often without stopping to question why their opinion mattered so much to me in the first place.

Looking back now, I see that much of this drive was fueled by my desire to prove to myself—and to others—that I was worthy. My relentless pursuit of approval had shaped my understanding of work ethic and obscured the idea that worth is inherent. It isn't something you can earn or prove—it's something you already possess. It's intrinsic.

The Adulthood Paradox

The values we learn as children often shape our adult lives. This, for me, meant emulating the passion and drive of my parents and the relentless pursuit of hard work, success, and achievement. However, the experience of adulthood can also bring a quiet realization that productivity alone isn't fulfilling.

For years, I equated busyness with worthiness. Full schedules, long hours, and the satisfaction of crossing items off of my to-do list became a perverse badge of honour. But, how was I going to shake the gnawing question: *Why doesn't this feel as fulfilling as I expected it would?*

In my early career, I prided myself on being the person who could 'juggle it all'. Whether it was staying late, volunteering for extra assignments or taking on projects beyond my remit were all part of my self-created narrative of hustling equals winning. And for a time, it worked. Promotions came my way, praise found me and, as my reputation continued to grow, I looked like I had it all figured out.

However, maintaining the facade of professional invincibility wasn't sustainable. Cracks inevitably appeared, culminating in a devastating encounter with my boss. *I found myself trapped in a room with only him while he manipulated my emotions, exploited my vulnerabilities, and took advantage of me.*

My focus on maintaining the "hustle" had blinded me to the very real dangers lurking within my work environment. I had unknowingly placed my sense of worth in the hands of this man, the one person I believed validated my efforts. While I did nothing to provoke or deserve his abusive treatment, my lack of self-awareness had created a vulnerability that he readily exploited. The experience shattered my self-confidence and feelings of worth, plunging me into the darkest era of my professional career. My achievements felt worthless and so did I.

Like many, I had fallen into the trap of equating a strong work ethic with 'having it all', including an inherent sense of value. I believed I was indispensable to my toxic work environment. But, when the abuse occurred, my dedication and hard work offered no protection, and I was let go. In a twisted bargain, I had tolerated manipulation and exploitation in exchange for validation; this stark realization, though painful, became the catalyst for profound change.

The Pivot Towards Fulfillment

The turning point came for me when I started to ask myself a different question: not "What do I need to do?" but ***"What do I need to feel?"***. This may not seem like a big shift but the results were profound. It forced me to reevaluate my relationship with work and success. It had me viewing my experiences through a different lens and instead of measuring my worth by how much I accomplished, I began to focus on whether my efforts aligned with my values.

I realized that finding fulfillment wasn't about increasing my productivity, it was about focusing on what truly mattered to me. This meant establishing boundaries, declining additional tasks, and prioritizing time for activities that nurtured me personally and professionally.

Hiring a professional coach was transformative. Despite my initial skepticism, my coach provided perspective, challenged my assumptions, and held me accountable. They helped me reconnect with my core values, ask better questions, clarify my priorities, and recognize my intrinsic worth. Investing time in coaching was crucial, as it empowered me to shift from relentless productivity to meaningful fulfillment.

Of course, my experience isn't meant to suggest that productivity and fulfillment are mutually exclusive. The challenge—and the opportunity—lies in finding a healthy balance. For me, productivity becomes a powerful tool when it serves a greater purpose, a vision that resonates deeply. The key, I've learned, is aligning my efforts with my inherent sense of worth, rather than using productivity as a desperate attempt to earn that worth.

The Power of Self-Awareness

It's one thing to realize that productivity without purpose leaves you empty; it's another to figure out what fills you. This is where the real work begins. For me, stepping back to evaluate my priorities wasn't just about asking myself better questions—it was about reckoning with the gap between who I thought I was and who I wanted to be. The process of digging into what drives me and what I value was messy, emotional and, at times, downright uncomfortable.

Self-awareness, as I have learned, is both the foundation and the fuel for real change. It's what allowed me to see how my childhood beliefs about work and worth had influenced the choices I made as an adult. I'd always thought I was self-aware, but in reality, I'd been operating on autopilot—letting old narratives about success dictate my decision-making.

During a coaching session, I was asked a simple yet profound question: "If you weren't trying to prove yourself to anyone, what would you want to accomplish?" The question stopped me cold, not because I lacked an answer, but because I'd never even considered it. The idea of pursuing goals for my own sense of fulfillment, independent of external validation, was foreign to me. It highlighted a fundamental shift I needed to make: from seeking worth through the eyes of others, to finding it within myself.

That simple realization brought me face-to-face with the uncomfortable truth that much of my ambition had actually been fueled by fear. Fear of being overlooked, fear of not being good enough, fear of disappointing others' expectations of me. I'd been so focused on external validation that I'd neglected to define success for myself.

Reflection for the Ongoing Journey

To truly embrace self-awareness, I had to confront my experiences with radical honesty; a process that included revisiting the abuse I suffered at the hands of my boss. This wasn't only a deep trauma; it was a stark revelation of my own vulnerabilities. It forced me to examine the uncomfortable truth: I had tied my identity to my boss's perception of me, and my sense of worth to their approval. This created a dynamic where I felt compelled to meet and exceed their expectations, leaving me deeply vulnerable to their manipulative and ultimately abusive behaviour. While my boss bears full responsibility for their actions, my vulnerability revealed the insidious nature of toxic work environments and unethical practices, and how they can exploit our human need for validation.

Self-awareness is not a destination; it's a journey of asking hard questions and sitting with uncomfortable truths. For me, this ongoing process, supported by professional coaching, involves regular self-reflection and a willingness to embrace growth—especially the humility to admit I don't have all the answers. In a professional context, this vulnerability becomes a superpower. It allows me to navigate complex situations with empathy and clarity. It empowers me to establish healthy boundaries without guilt and to decline requests without second-guessing myself. Crucially, it reinforces the understanding that my worth is inherent and immutable, completely independent of external validation or the demands of a toxic environment. This realization is the key to not only protecting myself from such environments, but also actively refusing to participate in or enable them. By recognizing my own value, I can no longer be complicit in a system that seeks to diminish it in others.

Worth As An Ethic

The concept of worth is not just a measure of self-esteem. It is an ethic; a principle that can shape how we live, work, and engage with the world. When we operate from a place of intrinsic worth—when we believe we are enough regardless of our accomplishments—it doesn't just change our inner experience; it ripples outward, influencing our relationships, our teams, and even the broader culture.

For much of my life, I viewed worth as something earned. If I accomplished things and was successful in the eyes of others, I'd be worthy. This transactional view of worth, however, is exhausting and unsustainable. Even worse, it perpetuates a culture where worthiness is conditional, where people feel they must constantly strive in order to justify their very existence.

Shifting to a **worth ethic** view wasn't easy for me. It required deep unlearning of ingrained beliefs and redefining what it meant to show up as a professional, leader, and human being. And it meant recognizing that this shift wasn't just about me; it was also about the impact I wanted to have on others.

When we live from a place of intrinsic worth, we create space for others to do the same, and this can have a profound effect on the environments around us. As I began to internalize my own worth, I noticed transformations not just in how I felt but in how I interacted with others. I became naturally more empathetic, more patient, and more willing to see people as they were, not just as they could produce or achieve.

I recall an instance where a team member was struggling with a project. In the past, I would have judged them for not meeting my expectations and taken over to resolve the issue myself. This time, I chose a different path. I concentrated on fostering their growth rather than simply solving the problem for them. I reminded them of their strengths, provided guidance, and then stepped back to allow them to find their own solution. The outcome was not only a successfully completed project, but also a boost in their confidence. Furthermore, their solutions provided me with new insights. This experience underscored a fundamental truth: Embodying worth as an ethic empowers others to recognize and embrace their own inherent value. It's not about being perfect or never encountering challenges; it's about demonstrating that everyone is inherently worthy and doesn't need to prove their right to exist.

Worth as A Leadership Principle

As I have continued to lean into this ethic, I've realized how transformative it can be in leadership. A leader who operates from intrinsic worth doesn't need to micromanage, hoard credit, or prove their value through domination or control. Instead, these leaders create environments where trust, collaboration and innovations can thrive. They seek out diversity, look to leverage and include it, and act in a way that elevates everyone.

As a project leader in high-stakes environments, embracing a **worth ethic** means prioritizing people alongside outcomes. It involves fostering a culture where every team member and interest holder feels supported and valued. You actively ask what they need to thrive—whether its resources, clarity, or encouragement—and create space for open dialogue. You encourage risk-taking, reframing potential failures as opportunities to learn and grow. Most importantly, you remind everyone involved that their worth isn't tied to the success or failure of a single initiative.

Instead, contributions rooted in intrinsic worth cultivate environments where people feel seen, heard, and genuinely appreciated. When people feel this level of trust and respect, their work transcends expectations, driven by intrinsic motivation and a shared commitment to the project's vision.

The Ripple Effect

The ripple effect of worth extends beyond individual actions. When worth becomes a core ethic, it has the power to transform entire cultures and systems—a transformation that is becoming increasingly critical in the face of rapid technological advancement. Imagine workplaces where people feel valued not just for their output, but for their unique perspectives and contributions. Imagine teams where collaboration is fueled by mutual respect, recognizing that each individual brings inherent value, even as the nature of their tasks may shift. Imagine communities where people uplift one another, understanding that our shared humanity transcends the ever-evolving landscape of work.

Building such a culture, especially in this era of accelerating technological change, requires intention, courage and a fundamental shift in perspective. It means challenging systems and norms that have long equated worth with productivity, particularly as automation and artificial intelligence reshape the very definition of 'productive work'. It means advocating for policies that prioritize diversity, equity, and inclusion ensuring that technological progress serves humanity, not the other way around. And it means showing up, day after day, as someone who believes and acts on the belief that worth is inherent and unconditional, regardless of the tasks we perform.

For me, there are still days when I fall into old patterns of command and control, both for myself and for others. But each time I catch myself, I have the tools to course correct. I remind myself that my worth is not up for debate and that the most meaningful accomplishments come not from my striving to prove myself in a world increasingly dominated by machines, but from living in alignment with my values. As technology continues to evolve and automate tasks, our human values—empathy, creativity, critical thinking—become even more crucial. When we choose to see our own worth, we give others permission to see theirs, even as the nature of our work transforms. When we live with worth as an ethic, we create a world where everyone can thrive—not because of what they do, but because of who they are, and how they choose to contribute their unique humanity to a world in constant flux.

Reclaiming Your Worth

It isn't a one-time decision. It is a continuous journey of self-awareness, reflection, and action. It requires peeling back the layers of past experiences, societal expectations, and self-imposed limitations to uncover the authentic value you bring to the table. This journey isn't easy, but it is transformative. A life where your worth isn't measured by the hours you log or the tasks you complete, but by the alignment between your values and your actions. It empowers you to lead from a place of intrinsic confidence and clarity, navigating the complexities of a rapidly evolving work landscape with your humanity intact.

If you've ever felt the quiet tension between productivity and fulfillment, or questioned whether your work truly reflects your worth, you're not alone. I've been there, and I've come out stronger on the other side.

The good news? *You hold the magic within you, just as I do.* We all possess the keys to success and to 'cracking the rich code' of a fulfilling life. You don't have to navigate this alone and can work to uncover your unique worth, align it with your goals, and create a roadmap to lead a life—and a career—that feels both impactful and deeply satisfying, no matter what challenges or opportunities the future holds.

The first step is deciding that you are ready to reclaim your worth.

So, if you weren't trying to prove yourself to anyone, what would you want to do?

Are you ready? You are WORTH it. And your worth will be your compass as we navigate the future together.

***

To contact Amber:

amber@thefeistypm.com

www.thefeistypm.com

https://www.linkedin.com/in/thefeistypm/

https://www.youtube.com/@thefeistypm

Jayne Johnson

Jayne Johnson spent years exploring various personal development methodologies before discovering Clearing Coaching, the ultimate game-changer, in 1983.

Inspired by its impact, Jayne became a Clearing Coach and has since had the privilege of helping thousands of people achieve their goals and dreams. Jayne's clients have included people from all walks of life, including an Oscar-winning director, NBA player and a 2-time PGA Tournament Champion.

In 1990 a Clearing Coach Teacher introduced Jayne to Robert Kiyosaki, best-selling author of *Rich Dad, Poor Dad*. This serendipitous meeting led to a personal and business relationship with Robert and his wife Kim, and in October 2000 they invited Jayne to move to Arizona to coach their *Rich Dad Company* staff.

And thus began an incredible journey Jayne never anticipated; not only coaching *Rich Dad Company* staff members but also taking the stage with Robert at his live *Rich Dad* programs.

As her amazing journey continued, Jayne became friends with extraordinary leaders in the personal development field such as Blair Singer and Dame Doria (DC) Cordova, and many other kindred spirits who are committed to making the world a better place.

Jayne is deeply grateful to all those who have supported her and her work throughout the years and feels truly blessed as she continues living her purpose to be helpful and of service.

How You Create an Upward Spiral of Success:
The 8 Elements of A Game Blueprint

By Jane Johnson

I began a committed journey into the personal development world in 1976. To be honest, my life was a complete mess due to my own bad decisions and poor choices.

My big breakthrough came when I found Clearing. It was a remarkable game-changer, and within the first year, I began studying to be a Clearing Coach. That was in 1983, and I'm still happily working with clients.

I'm grateful for all I've experienced and learned over the years and happy that I can share with you here some valuable ideas that I hope you will find useful.

Note: Included are exercises, and these three guidelines will enhance your benefits even more:

1. Don't censor your answers - fine-tune, revise, refine later

2. Write your answers on paper or iPad/tablet - don't leave them in your head

3. Don't be too serious - have fun!

WHERE ARE YOU GOING?

As humans on Earth, we are in motion much of the time, moving upwards, downwards, and occasionally sideways. Each of us is going somewhere, headed in a particular direction.

The person lazing on the couch for weeks is not going nowhere—they are going DOWN a spiral of failure.

To spiral upwards, the "somewhere" you are heading toward should be of *your* choosing; otherwise, life itself will send you somewhere, and it may not be where you want to go! So, consciously choosing your direction and then moving steadily along that path is a vital key to having the life you want.

WHAT GAMES ARE YOU PLAYING IN LIFE & BUSINESS?

I describe the concept of "**Game**" using the acronym **F – L – A – C**.

It stands for **Fun – Learning – Amusement – Challenge**. Any game ideally has these facets.

So now, let's go back to your choice as to where you are heading in life, and here is a very helpful question:

→ *What games are you playing in life?*

We are all playing *The Big Game of Life* but there are many games within the Big Game.

→ *Examples*:

The Family Game

The Coaching Game

The Investing Game

The Entrepreneur Game

The Writing-a-Book Game

The Spiritual-Evolution Game

The list is virtually endless because anything is potentially a game in this context.

Exercise: Take a few moments and make a list of the games you are currently playing in your life

Do this one exercise, and you will have made a giant leap forward in just a few minutes!

A QUICK INTRODUCTION TO THE 8 ELEMENTS OF A GAME BLUEPRINT

In my Coaching work, I love to empower my clients by sharing an incredible tool I call *The 8 Elements of a Game.* It is a powerful *blueprint* that will save you from many problems, losses, and upsets and support you in moving in an upward spiral of success!

Hold this blueprint up to any area of your life, project, endeavor, or goal, and you immediately have the most valuable information you need to move forward, knowing you are headed in the right direction with the right people and the right set-up to ensure your success.

THE 8 ELEMENTS OF A GAME BLUEPRINT

There are many elements of a game, but I have found that these eight are most valuable to know and apply to the games you play in your life. They are simple but will clarify and empower in the most profound ways.

Element 1: NAME

Every game has a name.

→ *Examples*:

Soccer

Tennis

Basketball

Monopoly

Mahjong

See or hear the name of a game, and instantly, you know at least some aspects of it. The name alone fills in many blanks. This is obvious, yet most people never think to name the games they play in life. It's not a common thing to do, but it is most certainly a POWERFUL thing to do!

Exercise: Look at the list of games you already made and give each one a very specific **NAME**

What Is Your Takeaway from Element 1, NAME?

Element 2: GAME LOCATION OR AREA OF PLAY

Every game has a location or area where the game is played.

→ *Examples*:

Soccer Field

Basketball Court

Monopoly Board

Mahjong Table

How can you play a game without knowing the designated area? How would you know if you're even on the field or off, if you don't know the boundaries of the field?

Every game you play in life, business or personal, has an area (or areas) for that game.

→ *Examples*:

Office

Home Office

Conference Room

Desk

Home

School

Neighborhood

Gym

You know the locations in both your personal and business games, but it's unlikely that you consciously think about them. Bring your game locations to your full conscious awareness, and you've immediately increased your power 10X.

Now, think of such successful people as Tony Robbins, Jim Britt, Robert Kiyosaki, and Oprah Winfrey. They all have the same field of play – Planet Earth. They're Global.

The internet has also given everyone the opportunity to play on a global field. You can be at home at your computer or on your phone and still be global.

Exercise: Look at your list of games, and for each one, write down the **LOCATION OR AREA OF PLAY**

What Is Your Takeaway from Element 2, LOCATION OR AREA OF PLAY?

Element 3: PLAYERS & POSITIONS/ROLES

Every game has one or more players, and the players have positions or roles in the game.

→   *Examples*:

Goalie, Soccer, Hockey

Center, Basketball

Pitcher, Baseball

Banker, Monopoly

Host, Mahjong

To play any game in life, you must know who the other players are, their positions or roles, and, of course, your position or role in the game. This is a key point because your chances of winning the game increase immeasurably when every player is committed to playing their position properly.

Exercise: Look at your list of games, and for each one, write down the names of the **PLAYERS & THEIR POSITIONS/ROLES**

What Is Your Takeaway from Element 3, PLAYERS & THEIR POSITIONS/ROLES?

Element 4: RULES

Every game has Rules. They give the game structure and integrity. Without them, you have people making up their own rules -- or any other form of disorganization and chaos.

In official games such as those mentioned, the rules are mandatory and already set in Rule Books. Also already set are the rules of a society or culture, the rules or laws of a City, State, or Country, and varying rules of morality too.

One of the positive aspects of the games YOU play in life is that you do have the option to make the rules, but once again, many people don't give it a thought. They get married, have children, own businesses, et al, but they don't consciously and purposefully create rules for their games.

These omissions play out badly in countless ways: *"I didn't know I was supposed to do that"* or *"I didn't know I wasn't supposed to do that."* The problems that result when rules are not set can range from minimal to devastating.

→ **3 Other Common Mistakes**:

1. Make rules but they are vague or ambiguous

2. Make rules but fail to enforce them

3. Make rules but fail to have the people involved volitionally AGREE to those rules

In sports, you have Umpires and Referees. In Societies, Police. In Corporations, you have H.R. That is a little joke, but it makes the point – you not only need rules; you also need someone who is neutral, understands the rules, and is authorized to enforce them.

The bottom line about **Rules** is that they should reflect what works effectively and constructively. Rules should promote productive actions while discouraging or preventing those that are ineffective – or worse, destructive.

Exercise: Look at your list of games, and for each one, write down a set of **RULES**

What Is Your Takeaway from Element 4, RULES?

Element 5: STATISTICS – HOW DO YOU SCORE IN A GAME?

Every game has ways you can score.

In sports and board games this is definitively established and not alterable.

→ *Examples*:

Soccer - ball has to go through the net

Basketball - ball has to go through the hoop

Monopoly – player with the most cash & property

Mahjong – player with the highest total score after all rounds

No matter the game, you must know HOW you can score; otherwise, you don't know how you can win. Without statistics, without something to measure, your ability to know if you're winning or losing a game is limited, at best.

To take advantage of the power of statistics with respect to games that you don't normally score or measure, you'll have to consider the reasoning you are using to determine if you are winning or losing them.

You are keeping score in the games you play in life, whether you think about it or not.

→ *Examples*:

Money, Annual Income

# of Sales Per Week

# of Cars In Your Garage

A PhD After Your Name

Your Child Gets All "A's" in School

Times You Exercise Each Week

Weight/BMI

# of Vacations You Take Each Year

As you can see, you can measure anything, so the value is in being present to WHAT you are measuring and HOW you are measuring it. That awareness gives you constant, reliable feedback so you know at any given time if you are going in the right direction, i.e., the direction you chose.

Exercise: Look at your list of games and write down what **STATISTICS** you focus on and how you measure them

What Is Your Takeaway from Element 5, STATISTICS?

Element 6: OBSTACLES/STUMBLING BLOCKS

Every game has obstacles or stumbling blocks. We don't like them, but the truth is, if there are no challenges at all, a game quickly becomes boring, and we lose interest.

→ *Example*:

Put a soccer team out on the field by themselves – there's no other team. The team out there just runs down the field and kicks the ball in the net - there's nothing to stop them. Imagine that in your mind and you'll see that, although you might call it *practice* or *fun*, it's clearly NOT a true game.

All games have some kind of challenge, whether it's a sport, a board game, or a game in life. Every problem, every glitch and bump in the road, everything that goes wrong when you're trying to accomplish something - those are the challenges and obstacles.

Some people find facing potential obstacles frightening, and they prefer to ignore them, a "strategy" that can lead to dire results. Some people believe that even mentioning a problem will cause it to manifest. I personally do not believe that. Communicating and confronting lead to solutions, as I see it. As the saying goes, *Fortune favors the prepared mind.*

What I have observed is that the self-confident person will welcome the opportunity to face an obstacle, assess the situation, find out what is wrong, and quickly fix it! A self-confident person is undaunted by obstacles and will just do whatever it takes to solve them and get moving upward and onward again.

Exercise: Look at your list of games and write down what the potential **OBSTACLES** might be

What Is Your Takeaway from Element 6, OBSTACLES/ STUMBLING BLOCKS?

Element 7: REASON(S) FOR PLAYING

This element is crucial. It's your "WHY."

Why are you playing the games you are playing? What are your reasons?

Of all the Elements of a Game, this is possibly the most important. Your answer is your driver, your motivation, and your spark, and the clearer and more cognizant you are of your answer, the more it will uplift and inspire you. You could call it your purpose or your mission. It is that force that keeps you playing, even when part of you wants to quit.

Consider the opposite, a person playing a game in life robotically, without knowing WHY.

→ *Examples*:

1. The artist who becomes a doctor because the parents demanded it

2. The woman who gets married because that's what her Mother did

3. The child who loves Science but Dad wants him to play a sport

Exercise: Look at your list of games and write down the **REASON(S)** you used for your choices

Consider your answers and then use these *3 Powerful Questions* to maximize the value of that exercise:

1. What is your ultimate objective?

2. Are you playing because you chose to?

3. Is it your choice NOW to keep playing or call it "done"?

What Is Your Takeaway from Element 7, REASON(S) FOR PLAYING?

Element 8: VALUE-ADD TO YOURSELF & OTHERS

In May 1990 in Los Angeles I participated in a personal development program called *Money & You*. It was a brilliant combination of business principles and personal development concepts. It was there that I first heard the term "**Win/Win**."

Win/Win means that the results of any game you play are somehow, in some way, directly or indirectly, of benefit to ALL players in the game. Everyone in the game wins in one way or another, but that might just be the beginning. Other people who are not directly in the game could also receive value.

→ *Examples*:

1. If you played a game and lost, but you also learned something valuable to help you win in the future, then it was a win for you too.

2. You create a game for yourself and your team in which you all volunteer for a charity: everyone wins – you, your team, the charity and all people they help.

3. You decided to play a game you called *Being a Great Teacher*; you finished your training and won that game. As a great teacher, all your future students also benefit, and those students might become

teachers themselves or will at least teach others informally throughout their lives.

Win/Win games potentially have no limit in terms of their benefit and value-add.

→ *Valuable Questions*:

1. How do you determine if a particular game in life is worthwhile?

2. What standards and expectations do you have for choosing what games to play in life?

3. How might the games you play in life benefit others, as well as yourself?

Exercise: Look at your list of games and write down how those games **ADD VALUE TO YOURSELF & OTHERS**

What Is Your Takeaway from Element 8, VALUE-ADD TO YOURSELF & OTHERS?

SUMMARY

THE 8 ELEMENTS OF A GAME BLUEPRINT offer you one way of continually moving in an upward spiral of success. Of course, there are many ways, but it is my hope that you found value in the information I've shared and that you can use it to create the life you've always wanted!

***

To contact Jayne:

JayneJohnson.com

www.youtube.com/c/JayneJohnson

Cheryl Meriot

With over 20 years of coaching experience, Cheryl Meriot specializes in helping high-achieving women overcome burnout, self-doubt, and feeling stuck. As a Certified Executive Coach and Clinical Hypnotherapist, Cheryl combines practical strategies with deep inner work to create lasting transformation.

Having worked extensively with physicians and medical leaders, Cheryl understands the pressures of high-stakes environments and the challenge of balancing professional success with personal well-being. Her warm, results-driven approach helps clients resolve conflict, improve team dynamics, and build the clarity and confidence to lead authentically.

Cheryl is passionate about helping women realize that everything they need to succeed has always been within them—it sometimes just takes a nudge to uncover it.

When she's not coaching, Cheryl loves traveling, reading, painting, and walking her two mini dachshunds, who rule the roost and keep her on her toes. Married for almost 30 years, she thrives on empowering others to break through barriers and align with their true purpose.

Helping High-Achieving Women Thrive.

Unwritten: A Journey Through Control, Chaos, and Coming Home to Myself

By Cheryl Meriot

The first time the song *Unwritten* truly hit home for me was during the wrap-up celebration of our cohort's first week together. Our graduate program was entirely online, and after days of intensive learning and connection, we ended in celebratory style, the faculty playing Natasha Bedingfield's *Unwritten* as our theme song.

As the melody filled my speakers, the lyrics hit differently.

"Feel the rain on your skin, no one else can feel it for you..."

I could feel the lump in my throat and the tears threatening to fall. This was much more than a song-it was a mirror reflecting my struggles, my dreams, and my fears. It felt like permission. Permission to let go of perfection. Permission to write a new chapter, no matter how messy or uncertain it might feel.

By then, my inner critic had already made itself very comfortable. Earlier that month, one of our first exercises was to name our learning styles. I remember typing out my response on the online platform, proud of myself for completing the task EARLY despite the gnawing doubts. For a brief moment, I thought, *"Hey, I've got this"*.

Then, I saw my classmates' submissions. They weren't just describing their learning style-they were citing academic papers. ACADEMIC PAPERS? The pit in my stomach was instant. *WTH have I done?* Did I just make an absolute fool of myself? For the rest of that month, my inner critic was on a roll, reminding me daily that I didn't belong, that I was too old for this, and that it was only a matter of time before everyone realized I had no business being there.

During the final wrap-up of our residency, as *Unwritten* played, something shifted. Those lyrics reminded me that my story wasn't a comparison to others. It was *mine* to write, one imperfect sentence at a time. It didn't matter if I felt like I was walking in quicksand; every step still mattered.

The lyrics felt like they were written for me—the controlling student, the controlling wife, the woman who wouldn't let go of a single ounce of control because the alternative was too terrifying. As I listened to the song again in my office, tears came. It was a wake-up call. As I let the song's words sink in, I realized it wasn't about perfection. It was about showing up, messy and human, and daring to keep going.

At the time, I didn't realize just how deeply those words would echo throughout my life. I'd always been the one who HAD to have it all together or at least appear that way. Control was my armor, my shield against the imposter syndrome lurking beneath the surface. It was the thing that kept me moving forward, even when it felt like I was taking so many steps back.

Control is a funny thing. To me, it was synonymous with strength. I didn't realize that it was actually a very deep-rooted trauma that stemmed from an early childhood memory that came out after my own hypnosis session during my studies. My mother had epilepsy, which was easily managed with medication. I only recall three events where Mom had an epileptic seizure: one after I had graduated high school, once in high school (the night I brought a boyfriend home to meet my parents), and when I was very young. I was 3 years old at the time; both of my sisters were off at school, and Dad was at work. Mom and I were home alone. Mom was lying on the floor in the kitchen, and I phoned Grandma to tell her what had happened. At that moment, subconsciously looking back, the 3-year-old me had to buck up and take care of my 33-year-old Mom. Ever since that moment, an unspoken rationale took hold that I needed to be in control of things, or disaster might happen…

Fast-forward to 2019. I was driving back from the store with my husband when my phone rang. My doctor's office asked me to come in to "talk." My heart dropped. I work in healthcare, and I knew what that meant. By the time we got home, I was already bracing myself for what was coming. I logged into the patient portal, combed through the lab results, and confirmed what I feared.

Breast cancer.

Control? What control? I told myself I was ready, but nothing prepared me for those words coming out of a doctor's mouth. The hours before the appointment were surreal. My mind raced, searching for answers I didn't yet have or even understand. No one in my family had ever had breast cancer. I've always believed that you can face anything as long as you have information. Having the information provided the control; control was my armor. But now, even with all the knowledge at my fingertips, I was calm on the outside yet felt complete panic on the inside.

I went into survival mode. I faced it head-on, armed with information and the incredible support of my husband, a circle of strong women, and a fantastic care team. Two of my closest friends had already faced breast cancer. They became my lifeline, ready to answer every question, share every insight, listen to every fear, and even occasionally share that bottle of wine or chocolate cake.

The hardest part? Asking for help.

I had to recover from a 7.5-hour surgery, and while my husband was incredible, he had to go back to work. I needed to ask for help, and I hated it. It felt like I was admitting weakness and not holding it all together. I was terrified of being an inconvenience to anyone. But there was no other way. I leaned into the discomfort, one vulnerable moment at a time. We made it through. I am cancer-free now, and for that, I'm profoundly grateful.

When I returned to work a few months later, it felt like I was catching my breath, only for the pandemic to pull the rug out from under me again. Between follow-up surgeries, constant monitoring, the global shutdown, and an emergency cholecystectomy, life didn't slow down—it piled on. But cancer, chaos, and the pandemic taught me something unexpected.

Resilience isn't about having all the answers or staying in control. It's about showing up, being present, and leaning on the people who love you. Vulnerability, as uncomfortable as it is, has a way of teaching you what truly matters. And for me, it changed everything. This shift profoundly shaped my approach to coaching, helping me hold space for clients in ways I hadn't before.

Imposter syndrome is funny that way. It whispers in your ear, "You're not good enough," no amount of past success can drown it out. Every assignment felt like a mountain, and every critique was a confirmation of my worst fears. I held myself to impossible standards, controlling every detail to hide the fact that I was struggling.

It wasn't until I began studying clinical hypnotherapy during the pandemic that I started to uncover what was truly driving me. Through the practice, I learned to reconnect with parts of myself I had silenced for so long: the scared little girl who thought she had to be perfect to be loved, the overachiever who tied her worth to accomplishments, and the exhausted woman who just wanted to feel like she was enough and be heard.

These weren't my enemies; they were my protectors, each trying to shield me from pain in their own way. Hypnosis taught me to listen to them to understand their fears and motivations. In doing so, I began to slowly let go of the constant need (or fear) for control and embrace a new way of being.

Fears manifest in countless shapes and forms, often rooted in experiences that magnify their hold over our lives. For Nancy, her fear of wasps became a daily torment after being stung at work, compounded by her severe allergy and the panic attacks that followed. Her phobia didn't just limit her; it isolated her from the garden she loved and the landscaping work that brought her joy. Each encounter with a wasp felt like a life-or-death crisis, leaving her anxious, embarrassed, and trapped by her fear.

Through hypnotherapy, we worked together to gently reframe her mindset and dissolve the grip of her phobia. Nancy's transformation is a testament to the power of the subconscious mind. She can now enjoy working in her garden and those of her customers with a newfound sense of calm and confidence, no longer weighed down by the overwhelming panic that once held her back. As she shared in her own words, *"I don't do the wasp dance anymore."* The freedom she's reclaimed isn't just about being outdoors; it's about reclaiming her life and thriving in the spaces she loves most. Hypnotherapy doesn't just address fears-it empowers clients to take back control and live boldly.

As I started helping clinical hypnotherapy clients, something unexpected happened. I realized I wasn't just guiding them through their inner journeys but also coaching them. Without even trying, I was blending two worlds: helping clients address deep-seated fears and guiding them toward their future selves. That's when I decided to pursue a life coaching certification to strengthen my ability to support others.

Marsha came to me at the end of her rope. She was in a bad place; hopeless and did not want to face another day. She was diagnosed with PTSD, bipolar, and depression since her childhood. The anxiety that she was experiencing was debilitating and was eating away at her. Throughout our time together, I listened to what she wasn't saying and challenged her to step out of her comfort zone, quietly or using her voice, allowing her to move forward at whatever pace she needed. This was about her.

Helping clients navigate transformative journeys is a profound privilege, and her story highlights how coaching, paired with hypnotherapy, can create life-changing results. While this client's challenges were rooted in PTSD, depression, and anxiety, the *process* mirrors the work I do with clients struggling with imposter syndrome.

Many high-achieving women come to me feeling trapped by self-doubt and fear despite their external success. They've "tried everything," yet still feel like frauds, questioning their worth and abilities. Coaching provides a unique space where I hold them capable-not by offering answers, but by partnering with them to uncover their own strength and clarity.

In our sessions, I act as both a guide and an anchor, ensuring they feel supported even when their confidence wavers or external pressures mount. This isn't just about breakthroughs in the room; it's about having someone who believes in their potential even in moments when they can't. Week by week, we work together to untangle self-doubt, find blind spots, and rewrite the limiting narratives that have held them back.

Watching my clients move from darkness into a place of authenticity and self-belief is deeply rewarding because I've been there, too. Overcoming my own imposter syndrome taught me the power of true partnership and the importance of holding space for someone to grow into their fullest self in the moment and for the long term. I was finally getting whatever "it" was. I knew I could help people, and it felt amazing!

And the inner critic wasn't ready to retire. Not long after finishing my clinical hypnotherapy and life coaching certifications, a high-level Medical Leader at work asked where I was planning to go for my executive coaching certification. My heart sank. Here I was, already feeling like an imposter for starting a new chapter later in life, and now someone was questioning me, whom I deeply respected. It wasn't that the question was ill-intentioned; it was that it hit the raw nerve of my own insecurities.

Still, I couldn't ignore the calling. I knew I wanted to do more than just help people untangle their pasts-I wanted to help high-achieving women, like the ones I was already coaching, break through their barriers and thrive. So, I took a leap of faith and enrolled in an Executive Coaching program at the one University that many of the physicians I worked with attended. My inner critic kept whispering that I wouldn't measure up. Would I even be accepted into the program at my age? I had no formal secondary education, so would the "life experience" be enough? Was I enough?

When the acceptance arrived, I was excited but also utterly terrified. I'd spent almost two decades working in healthcare with high achievers such as physicians, medical leaders, and medical directors. I helped them uncover their leadership potential and embrace their power, especially in managing conflict and concerns. But now, sitting in front of a blank Word document, tasked with citing papers and crafting academic arguments, I felt like a fraud. Who was I to think I could keep up?

Looking back, each certification (hypnotherapy, life coaching, and executive coaching) wasn't just about adding tools to my practice. It was about rewriting my story. Hypnosis helped me heal old wounds, coaching gave me a new sense of purpose, and every time I faced my inner critic, I reminded myself that my worth wasn't tied to perfection or anyone else's approval. And, most importantly, I wasn't doing it alone anymore.

Coaching became both my purpose and my mirror. As I guided my clients through their transformations, I was reminded of my own journey. The women I work with are extraordinarily intelligent, accomplished, and driven. Like me, they often struggle with imposter syndrome, perfectionism, and the weight of expectations.

Through coaching, I hold them capable, showing them that they have everything they need within themselves to succeed. In doing so, I remind myself that I am capable, too. Each session is a lesson in vulnerability, resilience, and self-trust. It's a reminder that we are all works in progress, writing our stories one day at a time.

Helping high-achieving women overcome imposter syndrome and its exhausting ripple effects is addressing the deeper patterns beneath professional struggles. For Lois, the challenges went far beyond career goals and stemmed from a lifelong habit of people-pleasing, blurred boundaries, and an overwhelming need to prove herself. Like so many of my clients, she was caught in a cycle of doing too much, working too late, and constantly fearing she wasn't enough, all while projecting an image of confidence and control.

Through our sessions, we tackled these underlying issues head-on. I created a space where she could safely confront the beliefs driving her behaviors and learn to replace them with healthier, more empowering ones. Together, we redefined what success meant to her, not as endless productivity or external validation but as alignment, clarity, and balance.

Coaching isn't about giving advice; it's about becoming a trusted partner, holding her capable even when doubt crept in, and reminding her of her strength when the urge to overextend herself felt overwhelming.

The result? A leader who excels professionally, prioritizes her well-being, and sets boundaries confidently. It was a privilege to watch her step into her power and let go of the dreaded "people-pleaser" role. Her story reminds us that overcoming imposter syndrome is about more than fixing what feels broken; it's about discovering the wholeness that was always there, just waiting to shine.

If someone had told me years ago that I'd be where I am today, running my own business, coaching incredible women, coaching physicians in our healthcare system, and embracing my authentic self-I wouldn't have believed you. It's not that I don't still feel fear or doubt; I do. But now, I see those feelings for what they are: reminders that I'm stepping into something bigger than myself.

Unwritten isn't just a song to me. It's a mantra, a reminder that my story is mine to write. It helps me get grounded before each and every client. Months later, whenever I felt overwhelmed with a deadline for school or a credentialled exam, I played the song on repeat…LOUD. The phrase *"no one else can feel it for you,"* reminded me that it wasn't about being perfect-it was about showing up, owning the moment, and believing in myself to figure it out. It's a call to embrace the unknown, to let go of control, and to trust that what lies ahead is better than anything I could plan. It's a reminder that I am enough just as I am.

To every woman reading this who feels like she has to do it all, be it all, and control it all: You don't. Your worth isn't tied to your accomplishments or ability to hold it together. You are enough just as you are. And when you're ready, I'll be here to remind you of that truth, one session, one breakthrough, and one unwritten chapter at a time.

***

To contact Cheryl:

Website: www.cherylmeriot.com

Email: info@cherylmeriot.com

Linked In: www.linkedin.com/in/cherylmeriot

Nina Buik

Nina Buik is a distinguished leadership coach with a wealth of experience in guiding professionals and businesses toward achieving their full potential. She holds a leadership coaching certification from iPEC and the International Coaching Federation (ICF) and is certified and proficient in several assessment tools, including the Energy Leadership Index (ELI) and Shift Positive 360. With a background in IT channel leadership, executive coaching, facilitation, and leadership development consulting, Nina has a deep understanding of the complexities of leadership dynamics. Her approach is both strategic and empathetic, ensuring that her clients not only develop essential leadership skills but also gain the confidence to implement them effectively. Nina's commitment to continuous learning and her ability to adapt to each client's unique needs make her a sought-after coach in the industry. She is dedicated to fostering environments where leaders can thrive and drive meaningful change within their organizations.e.

Lunch with a side of Transformation

By Nina Buik

Barb and I have been friends for years, so I cleared my calendar when she asked me to join her for lunch at my favorite Mediterranean restaurant in Chicago. We worked together for years and became dear friends along the way. I thought today would be much like our other get-togethers, talking about family, mutual friends, and how work is going. When I arrived at Turquoise, she was waiting for me and had a look on her face that signaled we would be talking about something much deeper than our usual light and airy exchange.

"For the first time in my career, I feel like I'm a failure," she started. I could see the tears welling in her eyes. "My new dream job has turned into a nightmare and I'm not quite sure how or even if I can turn it around."

I wanted to cry with her, but that's not what she needed at this moment. I simply said, "Tell me more." Those three words ushered a nearly one-hour purge of all that had gone wrong since she started her new job: "My new boss hates me, my team thinks I'm too pushy, and I'm not sure I fit in." I let her go on until I felt that she had unpacked all the negative energy that she was experiencing.

"Let's order," I said. At that moment, I was trying to deflect so she could get back to the center. Thankfully, she smiled and said, "I'll have the usual." We both ordered the chicken kebabs and some Turkish tea and then I asked, "How are things at home?"

"Well, don't you know all the right questions to ask today!?" Her sarcasm indicated that there was more to unpack here. Again, I responded with another question, "How are Al and the kids?" Barb looked up and away, and I knew what was coming. "They tell me I'm grumpy and working all the time and when I'm 'not working' I'm still glued to my phone." I could only reply with "Ouch!"

Now that I had gathered sufficient information, I had so many questions for Barb. I don't think either of us will forget that day. It was transformative, to say the least.

To set the foundation for where I was headed, I simply asked Barb, "Do you feel connected to the company's purpose?" She looked at me a bit confused, "Of course, I know that my purpose is to hit our numbers. I'm reminded daily of that!" Again, I asked, "Barb, do you feel connected to the *company's* purpose?" She looked at me with a resolute face and said, "Nina, the company is in business to make money for its shareholders and my job is to ensure that it does."

"I think we might be on to something, Barb!" I was a bit excited that I felt we made our first crack in the 'code.' "What do you mean?" she said. "Well, how can you be excited about what you do when you can't really articulate why the company does what they do and what their north star is? Making money is an outcome rather than a purpose." And by the intrigued look on Barb's face, I needed to offer her more.

"Let me give you a few examples of what purpose in business can look like with a few of my favorite and successful brands. Let's start with Dove. 'To help women everywhere develop a positive relationship with the way they look, helping them raise their self-esteem and realize their full potential.' How does hearing this make you feel?"

She laughed and asked me if I really wanted an answer or if this was a trick question. I laughed as well and said, "Okay, let's wait until the last one and then tell me how they make you feel…seriously!"

The next brand I gave her was Lego, "To inspire and develop the builders of tomorrow." Lastly, I offered her Apple, "To create technology that empowers people and enriches their lives." And I didn't even have to wait.

Barb jumped in and said, "I LOVE APPLE! I can store and look at my kids' photos and videos anytime I want to and I can FaceTime them when I'm traveling. I feel so connected to the people I love."

"That's great," I said. "Your passion just gave me the chills!"

And there it was—the answer I was looking for—the feeling that the brand's purpose gave her. Jokingly, I asked, "Did any of these purpose statements mention money?"

I asked Barb to go online and find her company's mission statement. So she took out her beloved iPhone and looked it up. *"Creating AI solutions that elevate human creativity, connection, and progress."*

The look on her face told me this was the first time she'd heard of this. This surprised me in so many ways, and again, I had more questions.

I realized that she was stuck in 'victim mode', and the world seemed like it was out to get Barb. And in her mind, it legitimately was…in her mind. I normally don't like to wear my coach's hat with friends, but in this case, I had to.

"Barb, you mentioned that your boss hates you. What evidence do you have that he does?"

She thought for a moment and said, "His body language. He's always crossing his arms when I speak, he cancels meetings with me more than he holds them. And so I took a step back and disengaged with him too."

What a mess, I thought. Poor Barb was making things worse by first assuming that her boss hated her and then disengaging from the very person she needs as an ally and the person who needs her to be his ally, too.

"How do you know your boss's actions are directed to you. Oh, and what's his name?"

This time, her response was like a "Duh" response from one of my kids, which made me laugh, although I didn't show it. "Because he, Raj, acts like he does."

"Okay okay, first, what evidence do you have that the truth that your mind is telling you is actually true and based on indisputable evidence?" Barb looked down and shook her head from side to side. "Second, let's try and look at Raj a little differently. You're relatively new there and the company is not that old either. What can you do differently to change the dynamic between you and Raj?"

"Well, I can't work any harder than I already am."

"Let me rephrase, Barb. How can you change the way you show up to Raj that could influence how he responds to you?" I could tell this time it resonated with Barb, and she was starting to realize that she has the power and choice to change things and influence behavior.

I could tell the wheels were turning, and Barb's distress was beginning to wane. Ahhh finally, I thought, we were having a breakthrough moment. While Barb is a dear friend, her situation was not new to me as a coach. As successful as Barb was in her previous role, it's completely understandable that she would be frustrated at her inability to successfully connect with Raj and her team.

"Barb, I know you have to get back to the office. What is one thing that you can do improve the dynamic between you and Raj?"

"I just really want him to know that I'm here for him and my goal is to make sure that my team is aligned with our mission." I sat back and let the word 'aligned' steep for a minute before responding. "Barb, the word 'aligned' is quite powerful. What came up when you said that?"

She looked straight at me and, without hesitation, replied, "I took this job because I felt an alignment with the CEO and the direction he is taking the company. I also felt aligned when he spoke of the companies values, how they hire and how they support the community. Basically, he 'had me at hello'. It was a true Jerry McGuire moment for me!"

"So what I'm hearing is that when you are aligned, the real magic happens."

When we realized what time it was, Barb jumped up and dashed for the door.." Thanks for everything including the check!" I laughed, and then a warmth set in. We made significant progress during lunch. Barb became more self-aware; she realized how important value and purpose alignment is to success and fulfillment at work and at home and that solely focusing on 'revenue' will not yield the sustainable outcomes she was looking for. It was very powerful, and I couldn't wait to see her again to find out if she had tried any of the strategies we had discussed.

Two weeks later, I received a text from Barb. "Lunch @T today noon," I responded simply, "K." But inside, I was so eager to hear from her. I wasn't sure if her shorthand text was due to excitement or more despair. I would soon find out.

When I arrived, Barb was sipping tea. I was surprised that she arrived early, but she appeared eager. We exchanged hugs and sat down, and I didn't even have a chance at small talk. She jumped right in.

"I couldn't wait to see you and share all the things that have happened since we last met." Her energy was a 180 from when we first met. She was smiling, her posture strong and leaning in, and she was expressing herself with her hands, unlike last time, when they remained crossed most of the time. I said, "Please, do tell!"

"After we first met, I did some soul searching and realized that I was being so hard on everyone, Raj, my team, my family and most importantly myself. Partly because I was trying to be someone that I've never been, forgetting my purpose both personal and professional and then dragging everyone around me down to my woe-is-me then angry level."

She was off to a good start. Self-awareness has to lead to any sort of transformation. "Then I pulled up the company's mission/purpose statement. And I asked myself, 'how does this make me feel'. The answer was easy, I was proud. Proud to be part of a company that valued it's ecosystem so much that it naturally made the employees, customers and vendors excited about what they produced. I totally missed this opportunity to engage my team and lead every meeting with our purpose or our north star."

While I didn't want to stop her rhythm, I did interject and ask Barb how she felt at this very moment. She looked at me with warm and slightly emotional eyes and said, "Grateful and Empowered."

She had set up a meeting with Raj. She said his response to the request sounded reluctant, but she said it was urgent, and he took the meeting. They booked a conference room, and when she entered, instead of taking a seat at the opposite end of the table, she sat next to Raj at the right angle of the table between them. She told me that before the meeting, she took several deep breaths, which helped her center herself.

"Raj, thanks so much for taking this meeting." He nodded as if he were indicating, 'go on.' "I joined this company because I was so excited about what we're creating here. The CEO gave me every signal that this relationship was going to go well and that I was going to accomplish great things. I put everything into this job. I have been working long hours, pushing my team, and canceling things outside of work so we can get our new platform off the ground. I realize that I've been short with you, the team, my family which I don't believe aligns with our values here and for that I'm truly sorry."

She said that Raj looked at her directly, which he'd never done before, and said, "Barb, I know you have a family, and I never asked or demanded that you stay late and work weekends. Your family should come first. Second, you have been pushing your team so hard that they came to me and expressed their concerns about your leadership. And lastly, I think you're incredibly smart and capable, I don't understand why you are pushing everyone away. I want us to succeed, but I want us to succeed as a team and none of you do me any good if you burn out."

Barb was taken aback by Raj's response. She had no idea that he felt that way.

She turned to him and said, "Why didn't you tell me this?" He told her that he wanted to but that she had become too difficult to approach, and he wasn't sure how she would take this information. He continued sharing feedback that he received from Barb's direct reports, and while it pained her to hear it, she knew this was exactly what she needed to hear.

After their meeting, Barb left for the day and headed home to process everything that Raj had shared with her. Emotions and words swirled inside her—not collaborative, burnt out, not balancing work and personal life, pushing my team too hard and away, complaining about me. Wow, she thought, "When did I become that person?"

At dinner that night, she shared the story with Al and the kids. They were completely enthralled, and when she finished, Al asked how this made her feel. Barb looked at him, laughed, and said, "Are you channeling your inner Nina?"

"Guys, I'm so sorry. You know how much I love you and appreciate you and I know I have work to do and I commit to doing a better job. I promise." She wondered how much damage would have been done if she hadn't spoken to Nina about all that was going on.

The next day, she called a team meeting. Everyone on her team showed up, and they all looked extremely nervous. She smiled at everyone and said good morning. Then she wrote on the board, "PURPOSE." They spent the next hour talking about how the work each does and the team aligns with the organization's purpose: "Creating AI solutions that elevate human creativity, connection, and progress."

They were all eager to share their ideas, which she captured on the whiteboard. Based on alignment, innovation, and practical execution, they chose the top three. She didn't want it to end.

When the meeting was just about over, she thanked everyone and then said, "Guys, I'm truly sorry that we got off on the wrong foot. I came here focusing on the wrong things, I was focused on working hard and making money. And in the process, I alienated all of you. I hope you'll give me another chance."

Hearing all of this gave me chills. Barb's self-awareness and vulnerability allowed her to repair the damage at work and at home. I wanted to know more! "How do you feel now?" I feel like I've had a brand makeover and transformed into the person I admire. I'm fulfilled with the work that I'm doing, and I'm happy." We finished lunch and hugged; Barb paid the check as promised, and I was thrilled that my dearest friend had turned her life around.

Barb and Raj made a great team and the rocket ship AI company they worked for ended up going public faster than anticipated. They were focused, communicated well and followed their north star.

***

Contact info:

www.globalfm22.com

nbuik@globalfm22.com

(404)285-4567

Afterword

Life and business are always a series of transitions... people, places, and things that shape who we are as individuals. Often, you never know that the next catalyst for improving your business and life is around the corner, in the next person you meet, next mentor you listen to or the next book you read.

Jim Britt has spent over four decades influencing individuals and entrepreneurs with strategies to grow their business, developing the right mindset and mental toughness to thrive in today's business environment and to live a better life overall. Allowing all you have read in this book to create a new you, to reinvent yourself and your business model if required, because every business and life level requires a different you. It is your journey to craft.

Cracking the Rich Code is a series that offers much more than a book. It is a community of like-minded influencers from around the world. A global movement. Each chapter is like opening a surprise gift, that just may contain the one idea that changes everything for you. Watch for future releases and add them to your collection.

The work of Jim Britt has filled seminar rooms to maximum capacity and created a worldwide demand. If you get the opportunity to attend one of his live events, jump at the chance. You'll be glad you did.

Become a coauthor: If you are a coach, speaker, consultant of entrepreneur and would like to get the details about becoming a coauthor in the next Cracking the Rich Code book in the series, contact Jim britt at: support@jimbritt.com

STRUGGLING WITH MONEY ISSUES?

Check out Jim's latest program "Cracking the Rich Code" which focuses on the subconscious programs influencing one's financial success, that keeps most living a life of mediocrity. This powerful four-month program is designed to change one's relationship with money and reset your money programming to that of the wealthy. More details at: www.CrackingTheRichCode.com

To Schedule Jim Britt as a featured speaker at your next convention or special event, online or live, email: support@jimbritt.com

Master each moment as they become hours that become days.

Take action today! Tomorrow is not your friend!

Make it a great life!

Your legacy awaits.

STAY IN TOUCH

www.JimBritt.com

www.JimBrittCoaching.com

www.CrackingTheRichCode.com

www.PowerOfLettingGo.com for 2 FREE audios

www.JimBrittAcademy.com